PIPE FITTINGS

 NIPPLES

 PIPE LENGTHS UP TO 22 FT.

 STRAIGHT COUPLING

 REDUCING COUPLING

 COUPLING

 NUT

 CAP

 STRAIGHT TEE

 REDUCING TEE

 STREET TEE

 STRAIGHT CROSS

REDUCING CROSS

 90° ELBOW

 90° ELBOW

90° ELBOW   45° ELBOW   REDUCING ELBOW   90° STREET ELBOW   45° STREET ELBOW   45° Y-BEND

 REDUCING TEE

 REDUCER

 UNION (3 PARTS)   PLUG   BUSHING   CAP   RETURN BEND

 90°   45°   STREET

UNION ELBOWS

 UNION TEES

 PLUG

 45° ELBOW

 TEE

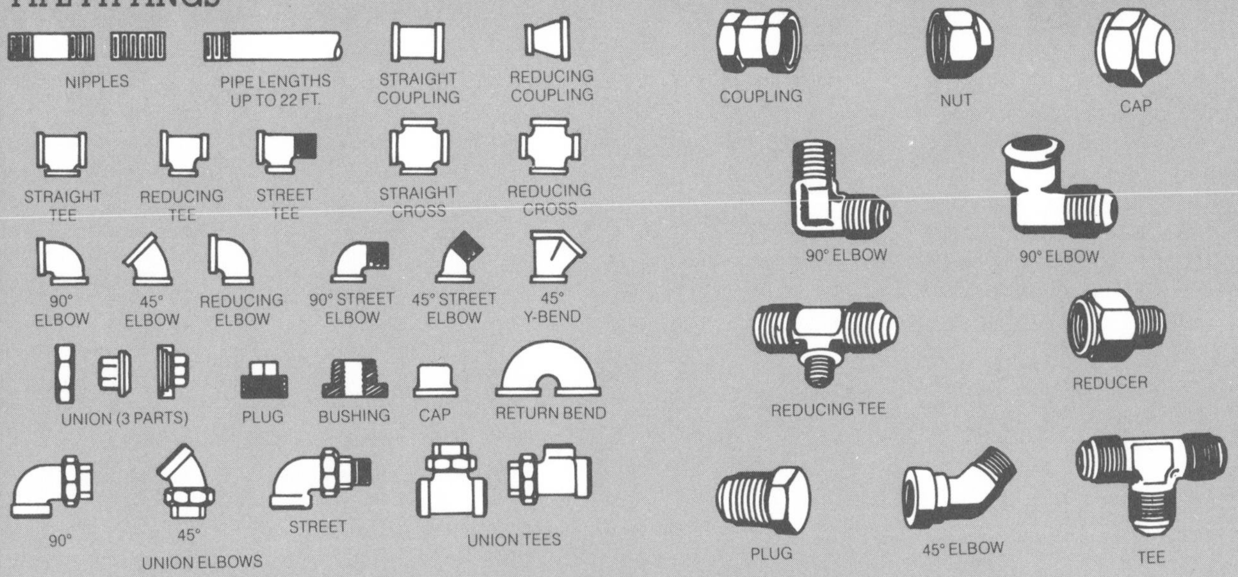

MEASURES OF CAPACITY

1 cup	=	8 fl oz
2 cups	=	1 pint
2 pints	=	1 quart
4 quarts	=	1 gallon
2 gallons	=	1 peck
4 pecks	=	1 bushel

STANDARD STEEL PIPE ((All Dimensions in inches)

Nominal Size	Outside Diameter	Inside Diameter	Nominal Size	Outside Diameter	Inside Diameter
1/8	0.405	0.269	1	1.315	1.049
1/4	0.540	0.364	1¼	1.660	1.380
3/8	0.675	0.493	1½	1.900	1.610
1/2	0.840	0.622	2	2.375	2.067
3/4	1.050	0.824	2½	2.875	2.469

WOOD SCREWS

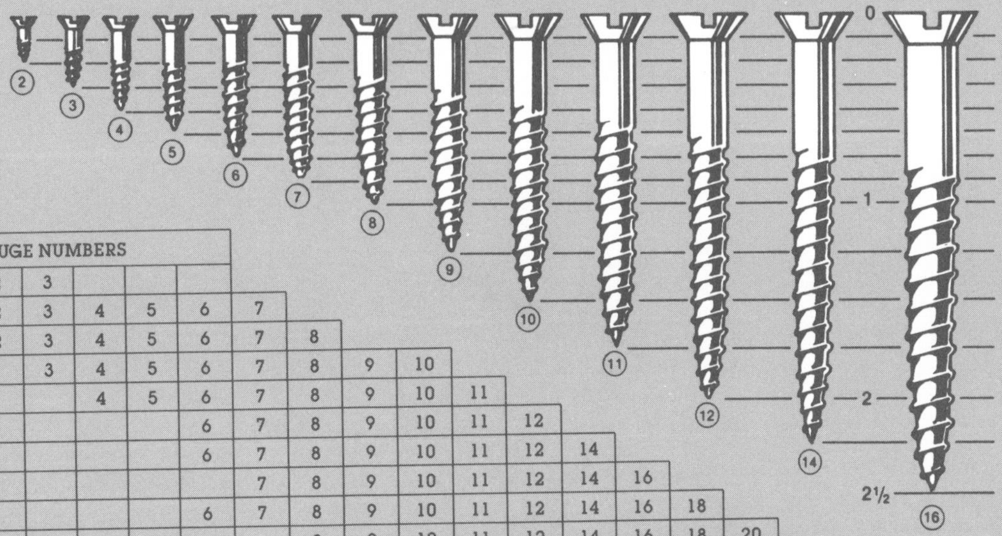

LENGTH	GAUGE NUMBERS												
¼ INCH	0	1	2	3									
⅜ INCH			2	3	4	5	6	7					
½ INCH			2	3	4	5	6	7	8				
⅝ INCH				3	4	5	6	7	8	9	10		
¾ INCH					4	5	6	7	8	9	10	11	
⅞ INCH							6	7	8	9	10	11	12
1 INCH							6	7	8	9	10	11	12	14
1¼ INCH								7	8	9	10	11	12	14	16
1½ INCH							6	7	8	9	10	11	12	14	16	18
1¾ INCH									8	9	10	11	12	14	16	18	20
2 INCH									8	9	10	11	12	14	16	18	20
2¼ INCH										9	10	11	12	14	16	18	20
2½ INCH													12	14	16	18	20
2¾ INCH														14	16	18	20
3 INCH															16	18	20	24
3½ INCH																18	20	24
4 INCH																18	20	24

WHEN YOU BUY SCREWS, SPECIFY (1) LENGTH, (2) GAUGE NUMBER, (3) TYPE OF HEAD—FLAT, ROUND, OR OVAL, (4) MATERIAL—STEEL, BRASS, BRONZE, ETC., (5) FINISH—BRIGHT, STEEL BLUED, CADMIUM, NICKEL, OR CHROMIUM PLATED.

Popular Mechanics

do-it-yourself encyclopedia

The complete, illustrated home reference guide from the world's most authoritative source for today's how-to-do-it information.

Volume 14

IGNITION SYSTEMS: AUTO

to

KITCHENS

HEARST DIRECT BOOKS

NEW YORK

Acknowledgements

The Popular Mechanics Encyclopedia is published with the consent and cooperation of POPULAR MECHANICS Magazine.

For POPULAR MECHANICS Magazine:

Editor-in-Chief: *Joe Oldham*
Managing Editor: *Bill Hartford*
Special Features Editor: *Sheldon M. Gallager*
Automotive Editor: *Wade A. Hoyt, SAE*
Home and Shop Editor: *Steve Willson*
Electronics Editor: *Stephen A. Booth*
Boating, Outdoors and Travel Editor: *Timothy H. Cole*
Science Editor: *Dennis Eskow*

Popular Mechanics Encyclopedia

Project Director: *Boyd Griffin*
Manufacturing: *Ron Schoenfeld*
Assistant Editors: *Cynthia W. Lockhart
Peter McCann, Rosanna Petruccio*
Production Coordinator: *Peter McCann*

The staff of Popular Mechanics Encyclopedia is grateful to the following individuals and organizations:
Editor: *C. Edward Cavert*
Editor Emeritus: *Clifford B. Hicks*
Production: *Layla Productions*
Production Director: *Lori Stein*
Book Design: *The Bentwood Studio*
Art Director: *Jos. Trautwein*
Design Consultant: *Suzanne Bennett & Associates*
Illustrations: *AP Graphics, Evelyne Johnson Associates, Popular Mechanics Magazine, Vantage Art.*

Contributing Writers: Rosario Capotosto, *Dovetail joints*, page 1728; *Kitchen door organizer*, page 1762; Rosario Capotosto and Martin Higgins, *Easy projects add spice to your kitchen*, page 1784; Rosario Capotosto and Harry Wicks, *Fine wood joinery you can master*, page 1716; M.J. Distefano, *Patio bug control*, page 1693; John Gaynor and Harry Wicks, *Jewelry you can carve*, page 1697; Everett Johnson *Jewelry box fit for a queen*, page 1702; Tom H. Jones, *Jewel boxes*, page 1707; Ed Kerr, *Termite control*, page 1694; Clyde Lammey, *Attaching legs*, page 1737; Wayne C. Leckey, *Joinery—a short course*, page 1710; *Joinery — a short course II*, page 1711; *Bonus tricks for your jointer*, page 1744; *Hideaways for kitchen and laundry*, page 1758; Alfred Osborne, *Hood for an over-oven range*, page 1760; Mort Schultz, *Electronic ignition system care*, page 1668; *Breakerpoint ignition system service*, page 1676; *Distributor tuneup*, page 1679; *Ignition cable replacement*, page 1683; *Ready your sparkplugs*, page 1687; E.B. Silsby, *Kitchen space aver*, page 1767; Tim Snider, *Kitchen projects and improvements*, page 1750; Paul Stenquist, *Electronic ignitions troubleshooting*, page 1671; D. Swanson, *Storage space in your kitchen*, page 1773; David Warren, *Turned-handle cutting board*, page 1789; David Warren and Harry Wicks, *Dowel joints*, page 1732; Harry Wicks, *Kitchen island you can build*, page 1752; *Hang-ups for your kitchen*, page 1779; Elma and Willard Waltner, *Colonial cutlery cupboard*, page 1755.

Picture Credits: Popular Mechanics Encyclopedia is grateful to the following for permission to reprint their photographs: American Woodmark Co., pages 1751, and 1773; Georgia-Pacific Corp., Great Woods Collection, page 1750; Sterling Publishing Co., Inc., CABINET MAKING FOR BEGINNERS, by Charles Hayward, page 1713.

ISBN 0-87851-167-9

Library of Congress 85-81760

10 9 8 7 6 5 4
PRINTED IN THE UNITED STATES OF AMERICA

Contents

Electronic ignition system care

■ ELECTRONIC IGNITION has arrived. By the beginning of the 1980s, every U.S. and foreign auto maker had made it standard on most models. Solid-state systems aren't all identical, but they have many characteristics in common. And they deserve care.

All electronic systems eliminate old distributor breaker points, the distributor cam and condenser. A toothed armature (Chrysler calls it *reluctor;* GM, *timer core;* Ford, an armature) on the distributor shaft teams with a stator or magnetic pickup—a small magnet and coil. They replace the old cam and points.

How solid-state works

That armature has a tooth for each engine cylinder. As one passes near the pickup, magnetism builds up and cuts off inducing a voltage pulse.

This slight pulse tickles the transistor switch in a "black box" so a pulse of primary voltage goes to the ignition coil. When it cuts off (as if old breaker points had opened), the collapsing field induces high voltage in the secondary windings. Fed back to the distributor cap, this goes through the rotor to individual sparkplug leads. The "black box" containing the transistor switch is known by various names, including control module, electronic control unit, and igniter. We'll stick to "black box."

What are the advantages?

Here are some of the advantages of electronic ignition:
• No point problems such as erosion or fouling.
• Dwell angle is no longer a factor. Dwell angle is the distance in degrees that the cam of a conventional distributor rotates when points are closed. It goes out of adjustment, because the cam and point block rub against one another and wear

down. But no parts of an electronic ignition distributor rub against one another.
• The whole concept of ignition tune-up is changed radically. Tune-ups are simpler and timing checks are needed only as often as you clean or change sparkplugs.

Manufacturers claim that because of electronic ignition and unleaded gasoline, sparkplugs give suitable performance for 20,000-plus miles.

It isn't service-free

But don't fall into the common error of thinking service is unnecessary. That isn't so. It's called for every 15,000 or 30,000 miles. Make these checks:
• When you replace sparkplugs, remove the distributor cap and inspect the rotor for cracks and burned areas on the metal terminal. Replace the rotor if it's damaged.
• Inspect the distributor cap. Wipe it clean with a dry rag and look for cracks, corroded terminals and carbon tracks. Replace a damaged cap.
• Replace high-tension cables if insulation is brittle or frayed. Test them for excessive resistance with an ohmmeter for the resistance values in the service manual. If you don't have a service manual, replace those cables that exceed the resistance values in this table:

Length of cable	Maximum resistance
up to 15 inches	10,000 ohms
15-25 inches	15,000 ohms
25-35 inches	20,000 ohms
over 35 inches	25,000 ohms

Replace only cables that fail. Don't replace the entire set. Cables for electronic ignition systems are expensive.
• Finally, check ignition timing. The conventional old method still works with solid-state.

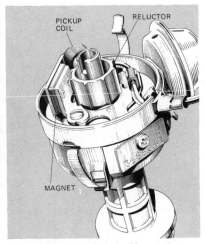

TYPICAL electronic ignition systems distributor differs from a conventional unit on the inside. Instead of breaker points and cam, most of the devices have a toothed armature and stator or magnetic pickup consisting of a small coil and permanent magnet.

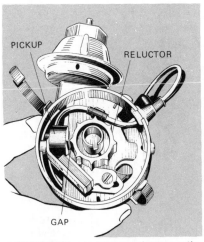

THE SMALL gap between the magnetic pickup and the toothed armature in an electronic distributor corresponds to conventional breaker points, but the gap never closes completely.

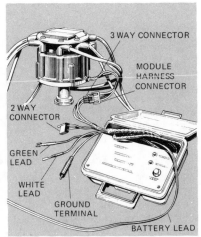

SPECIAL TEST instruments make tests simpler, giving go/no-go readings on a display panel. This one is testing a General Motors electronic ignition.

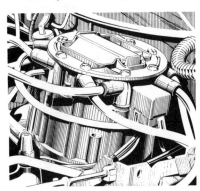

ELECTRONIC IGNITION distributors from GM are larger than those from other builders because they also contain the ignition coil and control module.

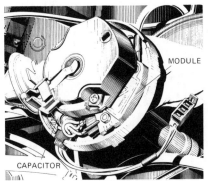

THE BIG rotor takes lots of space in GM's oversized electronic-ignition distributor. The capacitor is a radio noise suppressor, but the electronic control module is part of the modern ignition system.

THE IGNITION coil in GM's electronic ignition is a rectangular device inside the cap. A separate item, it can be removed and replaced individually if that becomes necessary.

Testing instruments available

Special instruments that make electronic ignition troubleshooting particularly easy are available. They present go/no-go displays on a panel. Although considered professional testing units, they are available if you decide you want one.

A universal tester is available. It consists of a basic tester and one of nine adapters—to make the basic tester compatible with the one out of nine different electronic systems currently in existence. Small hand-held testers are also available now.

In place of a special tester, you may use a sensitive dc voltmeter/ohmmeter, but only if you know how or have specific instructions. There are many potential pitfalls and a wrong connection can burn out the system—a costly slip.

In servicing the various systems, there are several points that may not be mentioned in instructions. Here are a few:

• You can get an overall indication of electronic-ignition functioning by disconnecting the high-tension cable from the center tower of the distributor. Insert a paper clip into the boot so it touches

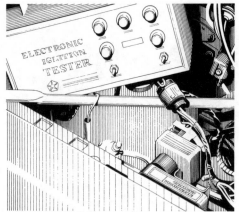

TO TEST CHRYSLER'S electronic ignition, plug the tester right into the electronic control unit. Once hooked up, it gives readings on the whole system.

SWITCHING transistor in Chrysler's system is on the control unit. It's "hot" when the ignition is on, so take care not to touch it.

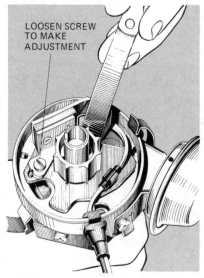

LOOSEN SCREW TO MAKE ADJUSTMENT

AVOID a magnetic metal feeler gauge in setting gap between the reluctor and pickup. Precision is important in this setting; follow the specs for your car.

the terminal and hold it about ¼ inch from a ground. Use insulated pliers to hold the cable; bare hands ask for a stiff jolt. Crank the engine. A fat blue spark between the paper clip and ground indicates a solid system.

Caution: With a conventional ignition system you can use a sparkplug cable for this kind of test. But don't do it with electronic ignition.

Holding the wrong cable to ground of some systems could result in damage from arcing in the distributor.

• Be careful around switching transistors that are exposed. They're "hot" and can set you on your tail if you touch one when the ignition is on.

• In GM's big, solid-state distributor, you'll find what looks like the conventional primary-circuit condenser. Don't be confused. It isn't actually part of the ignition system, but a capacitor that serves as a radio noise suppressor.

• If replacement of the pickup in a Chrysler unit is followed by hard starting, suspect the armature teeth-pickup coil air gap is maladjusted. A non-magnetic feeler gauge is essential for measuring this gap. A plastic gauge is preferred.

• Be careful around the pickup coil. Its wires are very delicate and split easily.

• A hairline crack in the pickup coil won't usually show up when you test the electronic ignition system. Hairline breaks widen under heat and can stop the engine. It will start when heat dissipates. If this is happening to you, suspect the pickup coil.

• Use sparkplugs recommended by your automaker only. Sparkplug gap is much wider than with breaker point ignition, and plugs have been designed with a longer side electrode. Trying to gap any other plug to specification will cause you to bend the side electrode to an extraordinarily wide angle, and lead to operational problems.

Electronic ignition troubleshooting

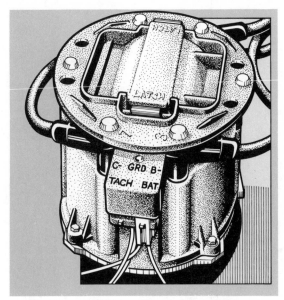

1 UNPLUG THE WIRE CONNECTORS from a GM cap before removing it. When troubleshooting, check voltage at BAT terminal.

■ THE NEARLY UNIVERSAL use of electronic ignition systems has totally changed the traditional tuneup. Gone forever are the days when a knowledgeable home mechanic could solve almost any ignition problem with a test light and a feeler gauge. Gone, too, is the periodic parts-replacement ignition tuneup. In their place are some regular maintenance checks and the sometimes complex fault-finding procedures that are used only when performance or driveability problems appear or when a vehicle fails to start.

Ignition maintenance

Electronic ignition maintenance should be part of your 15,000-mile checkup. Start with an inspection of the coil on vehicles equipped with an external ignition coil. (Most GM engines mount the coil within the distributor cap.) Look for evidence of external current leaks or oil leaks. Check the tower (where the coil cable plugs in) for signs of carbon tracking, arcing or burnthrough. Now examine the coil cable itself for split or cracked insulation, corrosion or any other signs of damage.

Replace both the coil and cable if the coil tower shows any evidence of electrical leakage. A slightly defective cable connection can quickly ruin a new coil. Replace just the cable if it is beginning to deteriorate but has not yet caused leakage at the coil.

Once you've completed your inspection of the coil, remove the distributor cap. The cap is retained by screws or spring clips.

Before attempting to remove a GM HEI cap with an integral coil, disconnect the wiring connectors from the terminals marked BAT and TACH (Fig. 1). HEI caps are retained by four screw latches; some late-model HEI caps have four conventional screws.

Carefully examine the inside of the distributor cap. Use a flashlight or drop light, so that you won't miss the more subtle signs of failure. Look for the carbon tracks that indicate current jumps. Check for cracks in the carbon button that joins the center of the distributor's rotor to the central cable terminal in the cap. Examine the entire inner surface of the cap carefully to make sure the plastic is not cracked. Replace the cap if it is even slightly damaged.

Check the metal terminals within the cap. If they are only slightly corroded, attempt to clean them by scraping with a sharp knife (Fig. 2). If they don't clean up easily, replace the cap.

Note the condition of the distributor rotor. It should be free of cracks, signs of arcing or burnthrough, and serious corrosion. Again, a small amount of corrosion can usually be removed from the rotor's outer contact with a knife, but deep erosion or corrosion on the rotor's inner contact is reason for replacement.

While the rotor is off, check to see if the distributor is equipped with centrifugal timing weights that are mounted directly under the rotor. These spring-loaded weights swing away from the center of the distributor as engine speed increases, changing the position of the rotor and, consequently, advancing the spark.

If the weights are corroded, clean them and apply a very small amount of white lithium grease to pivot points and other wear areas. If the weights stick in the advanced position, hard starting and spark knock can result.

When reinstalling the rotor, make sure it is

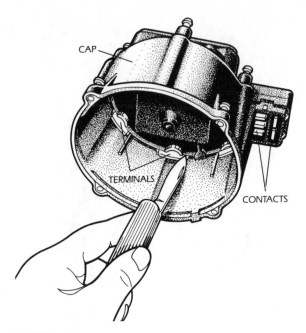

2 CLEAN CORRODED TERMINALS INSIDE the cap with knife blade, if possible. If not, replace cap.

fully seated on the distributor shaft. All rotors are keyed so that they can only be installed one way.

The tips of some rotors are coated with a special silicone grease. If you found this substance on your old rotor, make sure you apply it to the new one. You should be able to purchase the right compound at a good auto parts store or from the parts department of your dealership.

Next, examine the terminal connections on the top of the distributor cap. On GM HEI caps, you'll have to release the latches that hold the cable retaining ring in place. Each cable should fit tightly on or in its terminal, and the connection should be free of corrosion. Check for signs of burn-through, arcing or current leakage around each terminal, but don't remove the cables from the cap unless signs of damage are present. (On HEI caps, the wires disengage from the cap when the retainer is removed.) Plug cables on late-model Chrysler Corp. caps are retained by locking terminals and must be released from inside the cap (Fig. 3).

Clean the sparkplug cables with nonflammable solvent on a soft rag. Do not, however, remove any insulating lubricants from the wire terminals. Examine the wires for brittleness, cracking, insulation cuts or other signs of damage. If cable condition is generally deteriorated, replace the whole set. If one cable seems to have suffered isolated damage, replace just that cable.

Voltage leak tests

Chrysler Corp. ignitions operate at relatively low voltage levels, so cables can be tested for voltage leaks while the engine is running if misfire has been a problem or if the cables are suspect. *Do not* attempt this test on late model GM or Ford cars, as serious electrical shock and ignition system damage can occur.

To test for cable leaks on Chrysler products, connect the blade of a screwdriver to a ground with an alligator-clip jumper wire. The screwdriver must have a plastic or wooden handle so you'll be insulated from the current. Disconnect the suspect plug cable from the plug before starting the car and position it so that it cannot arc to ground. (Any metal part of the car is a ground.) Start the engine and move the blade of the grounded screwdriver along the length of the disconnected cable, watching for the telltale arc of a voltage leak. Don't touch the cable end or the screwdriver blade. Shut off the engine after each test, reconnect the cable and remove another for testing.

You can test the coil cable in the same manner if you disconnect one plug cable. Total test time must not exceed 10 minutes or catalytic converter damage can occur.

Ford suggests testing plug wire and cap terminal condition with an ohmmeter. With the distributor cap off and cables in place on the cap, connect the ohmmeter to a terminal within the cap and to the sparkplug end of the cable joined

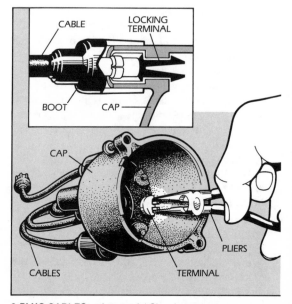

3 PLUG CABLES on late-model Chrysler cars are released from inside the cap by squeezing ends of terminal.

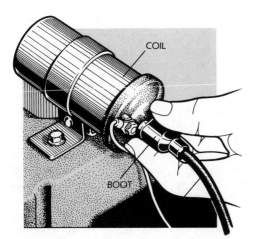

4 TO SEAT a cable connector properly, squeeze the boot to release trapped air.

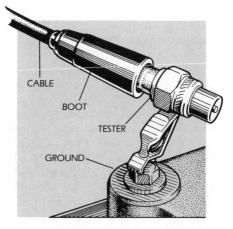

5 USE A TESTER to check for spark on high-voltage late-model Ford and GM systems.

to that terminal. Resistance should measure less than 5,000 ohms per inch of cable length. If it does, the distributor cap and cables are okay, providing they are free of cracks or any other visual damage.

If the resistance of the cable and cap terminal combined exceeds 5,000 ohms per inch, check the cable alone after removing it from the cap. If resistance still exceeds 5,000 ohms per inch, the cable is defective and must be replaced. If resistance is now okay, the distributor cap is the source of the problem and must be replaced. Check all cables, one at a time.

If you find that you have to replace the ignition cables, purchase a high-quality brand-name set that is designed specifically for your car.

If the terminals of the original wire set were coated with some type of silicone grease or other lube, make certain that the same coating is applied to the new wires.

Route the wires in exactly the same way as the original equipment, using all the original looms, separators and supports. When inserting wires with nipples into the cap terminals, push in the cable slightly, squeeze the sides of the nipple to release trapped air, then push the cable the rest of the way in (Fig. 4). It should snap into place. Make certain that the plug end of the new cable seats fully on the plug terminal. A poor connection at either end can result in damage to other ignition components.

Fault-finding diagnosis

The troubleshooting of specific ignition problems—such as misfire, no-start and intermittent die-outs—can be rather complicated.

Most procedures begin with a simple spark

test. This test will at least tell you if a no-start condition is the result of an ignition fault, because it can verify that current is being supplied to the sparkplugs. The test is a simple one, but the procedure differs for cars equipped with high-output systems.

To test for spark on Chrysler products and other cars with low-output ignition systems, remove the large secondary cable from the center tower of the distributor cap. Wearing a leather glove or using a pair of insulated pliers, hold the exposed terminal end of the wire 3/16 to 3/8 inch away from a good engine ground (any exposed steel or aluminum on the engine). If you can't find a bare metal spot, scrape a bit of paint off a bolt head. Have a helper crank the engine while you watch for the ignition spark to jump from cable to ground. It should be a bright blue, constant spark. If it's intermittent, weak or completely lacking, the ignition system is the cause of the no-start problem.

While the wire is arcing and the engine cranking, begin moving the wire farther away from ground while watching for a spark at the coil tower. If a spark occurs at the coil, replace it and the coil cable.

To check for spark on high-voltage late-model GM and Ford systems, you'll need a spark-test device. This tool resembles a sparkplug with a spring clamp attached to its base. It allows you to test for spark without holding the dangerous high-voltage cable. You can purchase this tool at a good auto parts store.

To test, connect the ignition coil cable (or, on GM cars with integral coil, one of the sparkplug cables) to the end of the tester and clamp it to a ground (Fig. 5). Then, crank the engine while watching for spark between the center electrode of the tester and the grounded shell that surrounds it. If you don't get a bright blue spark, the ignition system is not functioning properly and further diagnosis will be necessary.

To perform further diagnosis of an electronic ignition system, you should have a factory service manual for your vehicle. The manual contains specific troubleshooting directions for determining the cause of no-start, misfire and intermittent die-out problems. In most electronic systems, possible failures include the pick-up, which determines the sparking intervals; the control module, which triggers the coil; the coil; primary wiring; and in many cases, an engine control computer that determines spark advance. Some manufacturers use different names for these devices.

The second step in diagnosing most systems is a check to see that voltage is reaching the positive (+) side of the coil (the BAT terminal on GM HEI systems). This check is made while the engine is cranking (Fig. 6). Specifications for the amount of voltage necessary vary, but in most cases the figure is 6 or 7 volts.

If the amount of voltage available is less than that specified, there is a problem that is preventing voltage from reaching the coil. It could be a broken wire, a rundown battery, a failed ignition-system resistor or resistor wire, a starter motor that draws too much current, an ignition-switch problem or a fault in any other device that is part of the circuit between the battery and ignition coil.

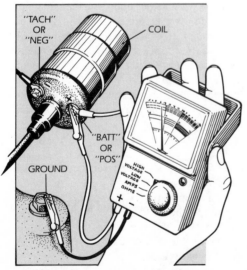

6 IF THE CAR WON'T START, make sure sufficient voltage is reaching the positive coil terminal (or the BAT terminal on GM HEI).

From this point the procedures vary significantly, even among the different models produced by one manufacturer. As an example of what's involved, we'll present the rest of the procedure for late-model GM vehicles with integral ignition coils but without electronic spark timing (those with centrifugal advance weights and a vacuum advance mechanism on the distributor).

If you found less than 7 volts at the BAT terminal of the distributor with the engine cranking, repair the primary circuit between the terminal and switch. If you found 7 volts or more, check for voltage at the distributor's TACH terminal.

If 1 to 10 volts are present at the TACH terminal, replace the module and check for spark from the HEI coil, using the test setup illustrated in Fig. 7. (When installing a new module, coat its metal base and the mounting surface in the distributor with the silicone grease that is packaged with the new replacement module.)

Testing the coil

To perform this test, you have to cut the small end off an old sparkplug boot. The boot is then used to attach your spark tester to the center terminal inside the HEI distributor cap. A voltmeter is connected between the TACH terminal and ground. The rotor is removed from the distributor, the module leads are disconnected and a test light, with its lead connected to the battery's positive post, is touched to one module terminal.

On a four-terminal module, connect the test light to terminal G. On a five-terminal module, connect the test light to terminal D. On a seven-terminal module, connect the test light to terminal P. Make sure you don't leave the test light connected to the module for more than five seconds.

As the test light is removed from the module terminal, you should get a spark at the spark tester. If you do, the module was the source of the difficulty and the system should be okay. If you don't, the coil is also defective and should be replaced.

If you found 10 volts or more when you checked "TACH" terminal voltage, check for spark at the coil output terminal by connecting your spark tester to the center terminal of the distributor cap, using the boot. Ground the tester and crank the engine while you watch for a spark.

Color coding

If you get a spark, check the color coding and routing of the wiring to the control module and coil. If these parts have been replaced, the wrong

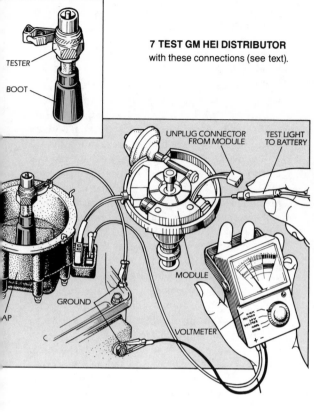

7 TEST GM HEI DISTRIBUTOR with these connections (see text).

TESTER

BOOT

UNPLUG CONNECTOR FROM MODULE

TEST LIGHT TO BATTERY

MODULE

GROUND

AP

VOLTMETER

A GM dealer would test the module on an expensive module tester before he'd consider replacing it. This is where the do-it-yourselfer may run into trouble. If you buy a new module and it does not solve the problem, you're stuck with the new module just the same because electronic parts cannot be returned.

Check ignition coil ground

If a new module does not solve the no-spark problem, check the ignition coil's ground. If it and the module are okay, the coil itself is the cause of the problem.

If voltage dropped when you connected the test light to the module terminal, check for spark from the coil as the test light is removed from the module terminal.

If spark is present, the pickup coil or its wiring is the source of the no-start problem. In this case, the distributor must be removed from the car and disassembled in order to replace the pickup coil.

If spark is not present when the test light is removed from the module terminal, check the ignition coil ground circuit.

If it's okay, replace the ignition coil and repeat the coil spark test. If a spark is now present, the coil was the source of the problem.

If it is not, your original coil was okay, and the module is the source of the no-start problem.

D-I-Y dilemmas

As you can see, the do-it-yourselfer who attempts to troubleshoot the system may end up spending more money than needed in order to perform the two substitution tests. The module tester that eliminates the need for this type of testing is very expensive. This will be the basic problem you'll run into over and over again when you are trying to troubleshoot advanced electronic ignition systems.

If you don't mind stocking an expensive spare module or coil, do the job yourself; after all, you may wind up using the spare some day. And, the savings in labor may outweigh the cost of the part.

But make sure the procedure you follow is the right one for your car, and don't even begin if you don't understand the instructions fully. A misconnected test instrument can damage a lot of expensive parts in just a few seconds.

ones may have been installed, or the wires may be misrouted.

If the module connector is yellow, the wires from it to the pickup coil should be green and white and the coil wires in the cap should be yellow and red. They should not be crossed.

If the module connector is clear, black or blue, its pickup wires should be green and white. The coil wires should be red and white. Both pairs of wires should be crossed. If the wiring checks out, the rotor or cap is the source of the problem.

If you don't get a spark, hook up the coil spark test as described above. With the ignition on, keep your eyes on the voltmeter as the test light is connected momentarily to the appropriate module terminal.

If there is no drop in voltage, check the module ground and check for an open circuit in the wires from the cap to the distributor. If both the ground and wires are okay, replace the module and again check for spark at the coil.

Breaker-point ignition system service

■ IGNITION SYSTEM tune-up includes replacing sparkplugs, reconditioning the distributor, and setting the dwell and timing. This program is essential to avoid such problems as missing, hard starting and excessive fuel consumption.

You can do the job yourself for the cost of parts alone—saving half or more of a professional's bill. Shopping around for parts saves even more.

You must have the tools

The first time you service your ignition will probably be the most costly, since you may have to buy instruments you don't now have. You will need a timing light and dwellmeter/tachometer. For the sparkplugs, get a plug gapping tool and gauge and a sparkplug wrench; for the distributor, a feeler gauge, distributor wrench, and distributor-tower brush.

We're concerned here with conventional ignition systems, not the electronic breed. Since electronic ignitions dispense with condensers and distributor points, servicing that version takes neither the feeler gauge nor the point file. And a simple tach replaces the dwellmeter/tachometer.

Here's the essential procedure for the breaker-point system:

Replace badly worn or damaged plugs; otherwise clean and regap good ones. Wipe off and examine the coil; if its case is cracked, replace it.

If primary wires' insulation is cracked, replace them. Be sure they're tight at the terminals.

Remove the heavier secondary cable from the coil tower by twisting and pulling the boot (not the cable). A badly eroded terminal or cracked insulation calls for a new cable. Brush out the coil tower and reseat the cable firmly if it's in good shape.

Now disconnect that cable at the distributor. Hold it with a clip-type wooden clothespin to avoid a shock and put the end ¼ inch from a clean ground. As someone cranks the engine, a strong blue spark should jump the gap. A weak yellow spark means the distributor needs service. If that doesn't help, replace the coil.

A molded rubber boot may be impossible to pull back. Then poke an insulated-handle screwdriver into the boot to contact the terminal and move the shaft close to a ground for the test.

Check the cap carefully

Unhook the distributor cap. Wipe it clean inside and out, and check for cracks, chips, carbon tracks and broken or eroded terminals. If it's damaged, replace it. If terminals are just blackened, clean them with fine sandpaper.

Remove one secondary cable at a time and check towers for damage. If they're OK, clean them with the tower brush. Be sure cables are good and each goes back to its own tower since

CHECK PRIMARY ignition wires carefully. They must be tightly attached at the coil terminals and must have sound insulation. Otherwise replace them.

CLEANLINESS IS important at the coil and distributor towers. A distributor tower brush will clean both, but you can also improvise a tool.

DON'T OVERLOOK the inside of the distributor cap. Even hairline cracks disqualify it for any further service. Wipe it clean before restoring it.

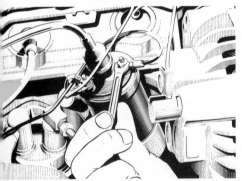
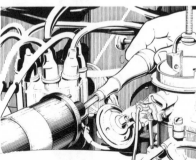
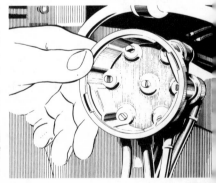

THE ROTOR carries high voltage from the coil to plug wires. Inspect it with care and always carry a spare.

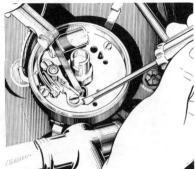

DISTRIBUTOR points are sometimes adjusted by twisting a screwdriver in a slot near the mounting screw.

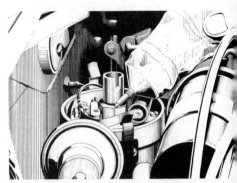

CAM LOBE lubrication takes a steady hand. One matchhead-sized drop goes on one cam lobe only. Don't over-do.

THE TIMING mark and pointer may be hard to see. White paint smeared on the pointer and degree marks will make your subsequent jobs far easier.

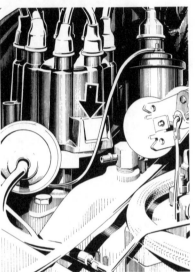

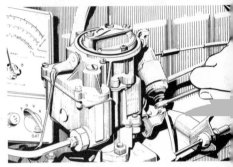

SET SLOW-IDLE speed at the carb before setting the dwell angle at the distributor. The idle-stop solenoid, as here, is often the means to use.

DWELL ANGLE can sometimes be set by sticking an Allen wrench into an access door in distributor's side. But don't forget to close the door.

confusing the firing sequence could damage the engine.

Remove the rotor from the distributor shaft; it, too, must be replaced if damaged. A radio-frequency or dust shield over the distributor can be set aside.

Find the distributor's direction of rotation by having someone crank the engine briefly. Then turn the shaft in that direction and release it. If it doesn't snap back, the distributor should get new springs and counterweights.

It may be hard to inspect breaker points within the distributor. To remove them, unscrew clips holding the distributor primary and condenser pigtail wires. Check their condition. Then unscrew the point assembly and lift it out.

Grayish or slightly rough points need only a pass or two (no more) with the point file. Wipe them clean with a cloth moistened with mineral spirits or alcohol, then reinstall them.

Get the point gap from a service manual, your owner's manual or the service decal in the engine compartment. Move the cam lobe under the movable point's rubbing block by having the engine cranked in brief spurts as you watch.

Some points are gapped with an Allen wrench in an adjusting screw. On others, you loosen the mounting screw, then twist a screwdriver in a nearby slot. Hold the feeler gauge straight. Be sure it's clean since dirtied points will fail rapidly. The gap is right when the points grip the gauge lightly as you move it between them.

If the distributor has a wick lubricating pad resting on the cam, replace it. Otherwise put just a drop of cam lube on one lobe. Too much will cause points to burn. Then reassemble the distributor.

Now set the dwell—the amount of distributor cam motion during which the points are closed. A smaller gap means the points are closed longer

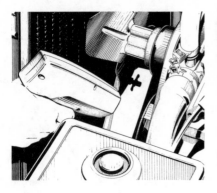 

HOOK THE timing light into the No. 1 sparkplug circuit and to the car's battery. When you shine it on the timing mark (far left), be sure to aim the light straight down to avoid any parallax.

THE VACUUM advance is removed by unscrewing it from the distributor's breaker plate (left). The arrow points to the lubricating wick.

and the dwell angle is larger. The dwellmeter will let you refine the setting you got with the feeler gauge. If they're closed too long, points may arc and shorten their life; if too briefly, the engine may miss at high speed.

Hook the dwell/tach's black lead to a clean ground, the red to the distributor primary terminal on the coil. With the engine running and warm and the instrument set for engine rpm, use the idle-speed screw or solenoid on the carburetor to bring idle speed to specs.

Switch the meter to **DWELL** and fine-tune the point gap. If the distributor housing has an access door, you can adjust the gap through it with an Allen wrench as the engine's running. If not, shut the engine off, remove the distributor cap, and reset the dwell. A wider gap reduces dwell angle. You may have to repeat the process several times.

Spark timing is adjusted according to the relation of an index pointer to a timing mark on the crankshaft pulley, block or flywheel. Connect the timing light. The heavily insulated lead goes to the No. 1 plug, often with an adapter between the plug and its cable. Some timing lights have inductive pickup clamps that grip the sparkplug cable. Other timing lights go to battery terminals—black to negative and red to positive.

Find the right timing mark. Those on U.S. cars are usually on the pulley or block. Some imports have them on the flywheel. Light paint or chalk can help them stand out.

Pull the hose from the vacuum advance mechanism and plug its end with a pencil. Start the engine and leave the transmission in **PARK** or **NEUTRAL**. The timing specification is based on an engine running at the specified slow-idle speed.

Aim the timing light straight down at the timing mark and reference pointer. The light's flashes should make both seem to stand still,

aligned with each other. If this doesn't happen you'll have to adjust timing.

Leave the engine running and loosen the distributor's hold-down bolt with your distributor wrench. Aim the timing light at the timing mark. The vacuum-advance mechanism on the distributor makes a good handle; grab it and rotate the distributor slowly. This will have the effect of changing the relationship between the reference pointer and timing mark. You move the distributor to bring the mark into line with the pointer.

Clockwise retards timing

Turning the distributor clockwise retards the timing, counterclockwise advances it. Remember that if the pointer seems to move farther from the timing mark instead of toward it, you're moving the distributor in the wrong direction. Reverse your wrist.

When the timing is right on the money, turn off the engine and tighten the distributor hold-down bolt.

Check your work now: Start the engine and recheck the timing. You may have to repeat the procedure.

Now check the functioning of the distributor's centrifugal and vacuum-advance mechanisms. Aim the timing light at the timing mark and advance the throttle until the engine is running at 1500 rpm (hook up your tach). The timing mark should advance as engine speed increases and drop back to its original setting when you allow engine speed to fall back to idle. If not, the distributor should be overhauled.

Reconnect the vacuum-advance hose. Again, aim the timing light at the timing mark and increase engine speed to 1500 rpm. The timing should advance itself farther than it did when you checked the centrifugal advance. If it doesn't, replace the vacuum advance.

Distributor tune-up

1. DISTRIBUTOR: 1. condenser; 2. points; 3. gap-adjust notch; 4. cam; 5. condenser pigtail, wire terminals.

■ ELECTRONIC IGNITION has come on strong, but there are still many more cars on the road with conventional distributors that use breaker points.

There's a lot more to distributor care than just adjusting point gap, and we'll cover all the maintenance on conventional distributors (Fig. 1) step by step. Servicing can be done with the distributor remaining in the engine, but it should be removed for bench work if a serious problem is revealed. Servicing is done to avoid or overcome such engine problems as hard starting, stalling, missing, and excessive fuel consumption.

1. Remove cables from the distributor towers. Grasp the cable's boot, twist and pull. Do not pull on the cable itself.

As you take each cable from its respective tower, mark the cable and tower with some identifying number or letter. Each cable has to be returned to its respective tower to prevent damage to the engine.

Use clip-type clothespins or pieces of masking tape on which you've written an identifying number to mark cables. To identify towers, apply a piece of masking tape to each.

Remember: The tower and its respective cable must have the same identifying mark.

2. Remove the distributor cap. For the most part, caps are held by either a pair of clips or holding devices having slotted screw-type heads.

If clips are used, insert the tip of a screwdriver behind each clip, snapping the clip off the cap (Fig. 2).

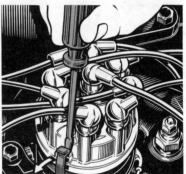

2. CLIP-TYPE fasteners for distributor cap are snapped open to remove cap for access.

3. INSPECT all terminals and the center contact inside the cap. They must be clean and not worn.

4. DISTRIBUTOR rotor is removed and inspected. Replace if it's cracked or has corroded terminals.

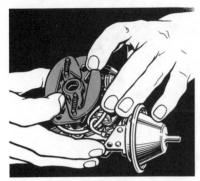

5. TO TEST centrifugal advance unit, spread counterweights to their limit and let them snap closed.

6. CHECK wires: primary lead (1) and condenser pigtail (2). Arrow shows connector for wires.

7. REMOVE point assembly held at mountings (1) and (2). Note condenser mounting screw (3).

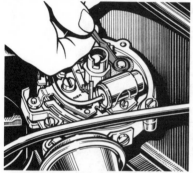

8. TO REPLACE cam lubricating wick, release small lock-type washer with a screwdriver.

9. CAM MUST not be overlubricated. With cam lubricating wick, do not lubricate cam at all.

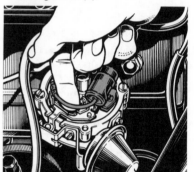

10. CONDENSER pigtail and primary wires should be routed so they don't touch moving parts.

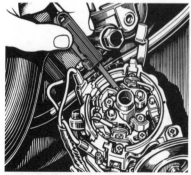

11. FEELER gauge must be held properly for accuracy. This distributor uses two sets of points.

12. POINT GAP is set accurately by means of the adjustment notch in the point assembly.

13. SQUEEZE BOOTS as you replace the wires to release trapped air for good connection.

If slotted heads are used, insert a screwdriver into the slot. Turn to disengage the latch.

3. Examine the outside and inside of the cap closely. On the outside look for visible cracks, broken towers and carbon tracks. A carbon track is a trail of soot running along the cap. It signifies a hairline crack.

On the inside look for burned or badly cor-roded terminals, worn center contact and carbon tracks (Fig. 3).

4. Replace the cap if there is reason to suspect damage. Make sure when buying a new cap that it's the one for your car.

If you replace the cap, lay new and old caps side by side so markings and distinctive features are aligned. Transfer pieces of masking tape with identifying numbers from the towers of the old cap to the respective towers of the new cap.

5. If the old cap can be reused, wipe it clean with paper towels or a clean rag. Polish terminals which are coated with a thin layer of carbon or are slightly corroded by rubbing lightly with a piece of sandpaper.

Clean out each tower. You can use a professional-type distributor tower cleaning tool, which can be purchased in an auto supply store, or a small, round wire brush.

6. Take the rotor from the top of the distributor shaft. For the most part, there are two kinds. One type can simply be pulled off (Fig. 4). The other, which resembles a cap that seems to cover the entire distributor, is held by two screws that have to be removed.

7. Examine the rotor as carefully as you did the distributor. Look for cracks, carbon tracks, breaks, and a burned, corroded or broken metal terminal. Replace a rotor showing even slight damage. Be sure you get the one for your distributor. Not all rotors are the same size although they may be of the same configuration.

8. You may see some sort of cover over the distributor. In some cars this is a radio frequency interference (RFI) shield; it's a dust shield. But it has no bearing on distributor performance. Remove screws and then lift each half of the shield off.

9. Find out if the centrifugal advance mechanism is functioning properly. The centrifugal advance is the mechanism, consisting of counterweights and springs, that alters ignition timing by means of centrifugal force as engine speed varies.

The mechanism may be in full view, sitting on top of the distributor shaft. If it is, twist the two parts of the assembly until they are wide apart (Fig. 5). Let them go.

If the parts spring back together, you can proceed to the next step. If not, then the reason for the trouble—whether weak springs, a damaged mechanism or binding distributor shaft or bearings—should be found.

In other distributors, the centrifugal advance is positioned beneath the breaker plate, and you can't get to it. To find out if it's working properly, place the rotor back on the distributor shaft, twist the shaft about 5° in the direction of rotation, and let go. Action should be snappy.

The direction of rotation can be determined by having someone crank the engine for a second or two as you watch in which direction the rotor turns.

10. The spark advance mechanism should be tested to get an idea if it's working. The unit is a vacuum-operated chamber which is usually attached to the outside of the distributor (Fig. 5). It controls ignition timing during acceleration, causing spark to occur earlier.

Place your finger against the rear of the distributor breaker point assembly, pressing against the assembly in a direction which is opposite that of shaft rotation. This causes the distributor point base plate (breaker plate) to turn.

At the same time, hold the tip of your finger tightly against the opening of the spark advance chamber to which the vacuum hose was attached (remove the hose). Release the point assembly. The breaker plate should not move. If it does, replace the spark advance chamber.

Now remove your finger from the opening. The breaker plate should swivel smartly back to its original position. If it doesn't, the cause of the bind (weak spark advance unit or damage to the distributor itself) should be found.

11. Remove the breaker points from the distributor for examination. It is difficult in most cases to get a good look at the points with them still in the distributor.

Loosen the terminal screw on the breaker point assembly and remove the coil-to-distributor primary wire. At this point, let's stop a minute and give that primary wire a very close examination, especially where it enters the distributor housing (Fig. 6). You may spot a potential problem which, when it occurs, baffles car owners and mechanics alike.

A reason for sudden ignition failure, leading to stalling when the car is on the road, is worn primary wire insulation. Exposed bare wires short themselves against the metal distributor housing, which interrupts the flow of current.

Replace a badly frayed coil-to-distributor primary wire.

Also disconnect the condenser pigtail wire between the condenser and breaker points. If this wire is damaged, replace the condenser.

12. There is no need to install new distributor points unless they are needed (Fig. 7). Spread the two points apart and examine surfaces. If points have an overall gray color and/or show slight roughness or pitting, pass a clean fine-cut contact point file between them one time only. Wipe point surfaces with a clean lint-free rag which has been moistened with alcohol.

Cautions: Do not try to file points smooth. The purpose of filing is to remove scale and dirt. Be sure the file is neither greasy nor dirty since contaminants will be passed on to point surfaces.

And don't use emery cloth or sandpaper for cleaning points. Particles will embed themselves, causing arcing and rapid deterioration of point surfaces.

13. If distributor points are severely burned or very rough, replace them with a new set. However, there is usually a reason why points get this way if they have failed within, say, 10,000 miles. Unless the condition is found and corrected, new points may also fail prematurely.

The usual causes for rapid point failure include a weak condenser, weak contact point spring tension, improper point gapping, an over-lubricated distributor cam that is tossing lubricant onto point surfaces, malfunctioning voltage regulator, bad resistor, and oil or crankcase vapors that are seeping into the distributor housing and affecting points.

14. If you have to replace contact points, replace the condenser, too. The two work as a team. Unscrew the condenser mounting screw and lift the part out of the distributor (Fig. 7).

15. Wipe the breaker plate clean.

16. Lubricate the cam. Some distributors are equipped with a cam lubricator wick that you should replace with a new one (Fig. 8). Do not relubricate an old wick. You'll cause more trouble than a new one is worth.

Distributors that don't have wick lubricators should have one drop of distributor cam lubricant applied to *one* lobe of the cam (Fig. 9). The drop of lubricant should be equivalent in size to the head of a match.

17. Place the condenser into position on the breaker plate and tighten its mounting screw.

18. Install the breaker point assembly, screwing it securely to the breaker plate.

19. Now, reconnect the primary ignition and condenser pigtail wires, but make certain that the terminal clips aren't in contact with the breaker plate. This will cause a short. Tuck the two wires carefully into the housing, but see to it that they aren't touching any moving parts (Fig. 10).

20. Gap points, using a distributor point (flat) feeler gauge. The purpose of gapping is to bring point adjustment inside the ball park. When the distributor is reassembled and buttoned up, points should be finely adjusted by means of a dwell meter.

To gap points, set the rubbing block of the breaker point assembly on a lobe (raised part) of the cam. You may have to tease the cam into place by having someone in the car crank the ignition in short spurts until the rubbing block ends up resting on a high point of the cam.

You might want to consider the purchase of a remote starter switch, which allows you to crank the engine from beneath the hood. It's a handy device to have around, especially if there's no one available to give you a hand.

In order to gap points, you will need the specification for your distributor. This may be obtained from a tune-up decal which may be pasted somewhere in the engine compartment. You can also get the spec from a service manual or owner's manual.

The gap specification is generally given as a range—for example, .016–.019 inch. If points are new, gap them to the maximum specification (.019 inch). If points are used, gap them to the minimum specification (.016 inch).

Use a feeler gauge that's the same thickness as the specified point gap setting (.016 inch, for instance). Insert the gauge between the points.

Caution: Make sure the feeler gauge is absolutely clean. Hold the gauge straight. Don't twist it. The measurement will not be accurate if you do (Fig. 11).

If you don't feel slight resistance on the gauge as you slide it back and forth between points (if the gauge moves too loosely or rubs hard), points have to be adjusted in one of two ways. One way is by means of an adjustment notch in the point assembly, near a mounting screw. Loosen this screw, insert a screwdriver in the notch, and twist until points open or close to the desired setting (Fig. 12). Keep the gauge in position, testing until the proper gap is attained. Then tighten the mounting screw and doublecheck to make certain the gap is as specified. The point assembly may instead have a point adjustment screw. Insert an Allen wrench in the screw head and turn the screw until the desired setting is attained. Keep the feeler gauge in place, testing as you go along.

21. Finish distributor tune-up by installing the RFI or dust shield, if one is used, and rotor. If the rotor is the type that fits on the distributor shaft without being held by screws, apply two or three drops of SAE 10 or 20 engine oil directly to the inside of the distributor shaft. Make certain no oil drips into the distributor housing.

Reinstall the distributor cap securely and replace cables. Be certain that each cable is inserted into its proper tower.

To seat cables properly, squeeze cable boots as you insert the terminal into the tower to release trapped air (Fig. 13). Make sure cables are firmly seated. If they aren't, arcing may occur, damaging the distributor cap and terminals.

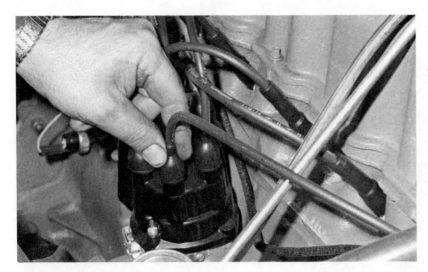

THINK OF THE BOOT as a handle: Pull on it never on the cable itself. Numbered tape patches identify the individual cables and the right location for their terminals. Sparkplug pliers make removal of the cables easier and prevent any damage to them. The tool isn't expensive.

Ignition cable replacement

■ NOTHING LASTS FOREVER—not even the heavy cables leading from each of your engine's distributor-cap towers to respective sparkplugs. These cables carry high voltage (about 20,000 volts) to the plugs. If they fall down on the job, your engine may misfire.

As for a cable, the way in which misfire occurs depends largely on the degree of damage to the cable and the amount of resistance offered by engine compression.

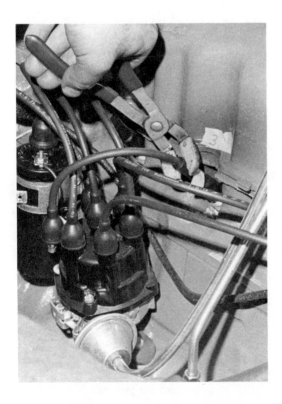

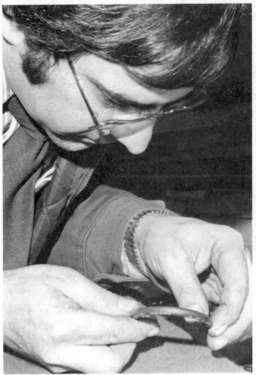

STUDY CABLES closely for cracks or frayed areas and bend them gently to check for brittleness.

That is why one engine may misfire only when the engine is under load; another at all throttle speeds, and a third only when the air is damp. (Moisture is an ideal conductor; a cable beginning to fail may do so only in the presence of moisture.)

In a sound electrical system, the path of least resistance, the path over which electricity finds it easiest to flow, is across sparkplug electrodes. However, when a high-voltage cable develops a defect in its insulation, this path may be through the insulation to a ground presented by the engine near which the cable passes. If the cable "sparks," less or no current will be available at the sparkplug for *it* to spark.

When engine misfire occurs—no matter under what conditions—think cables! Repairing "something else" when it isn't the problem costs money for nothing.

Many factors you can't control affect the life of high-tension cables. Age, heat, cold, oil and grease attack insulation, making it brittle and causing it to crack. Where salt is used on roads during winter, cables can become coated with salt spray. A salt-coated, cracked cable will short out since salt is a conductor.

Watch for corona, too

Corona, the magnetic field surrounding high-tension wiring, is another phenomenon affecting cables. The magnetic field created by high-current surging is so strong that it breaks down oxygen, converting it to ozone which is particularly detrimental to rubber insulation.

Disconnect and examine one high-tension cable at a time. At the distributor cap, grasp a terminal boot and disconnect it from the tower with a twisting, pulling motion. You should never pull the cable itself. Sloppy handling of cables is the main reason they fail before their time.

When the cable has been disconnected from the tower, trace the cable to its sparkplug. The process of relating the distributor-cap tower to its cable and then tracing each cable to the specific sparkplug it serves is very important.

For a simple way to identify components, use masking tape. Suppose the cable you disconnect serves the first sparkplug on the left-hand (driver's-side) bank of a V8 engine. Snip off three pieces of masking tape and write on each the designation "L1," meaning first plug left side. Stick a strip on the distributor-cap tower, another around the cable and the third near the sparkplug. Disconnect the cable at the plug—grasp and pull the boot only, not the wire.

A good tool you might consider buying is a sparkplug-cable pliers. It helps prevent cable damage and lets you grasp the terminal boot firmly. The "scissor-grip" permits a tight hold as you pull off the boot.

With the cable disconnected and all components identified, clean the cable with a kerosene-moistened cloth. Wipe it dry with a clean cloth. Now, bend the cable over its entire length. Discard it if cracks show, if it is chafed or if insulation is brittle.

Also check the cable terminals. If one is black, it tells you there has been a poor connection with either the plug terminal or the distributor cap. Secondary current has been forced to arc across the gap.

If this arcing has eaten at the cable's terminal, the cable should be replaced. If there has merely been carbon deposited on the terminal, wipe it clean and be sure the contact is a good one when you restore the cable.

For your inspection, you can often slide the

FAULTY CABLES CAN CAUSE ENGINE MISFIRE

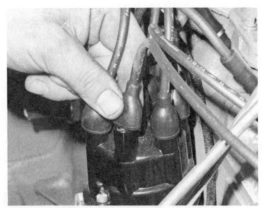

SEAT CABLES by pushing lightly down on them as you squeeze the boot to let trapped air out.

TO PROBE A cable, disconnect it from the plug and put that end where it won't ground out (upper arrow). Then hook the probing instrument to a good ground (lower arrow). With the engine running, probe along the cable's full length; any spark jumping to the screwdriver means the cable is faulty.

AN OHMMETER CHECKS a cable's resistance. Arrows show where the meter's probes are connected.

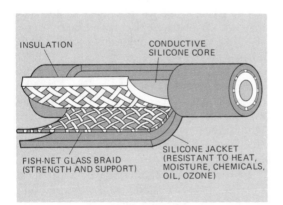

INSULATION

CONDUCTIVE SILICONE CORE

FISH-NET GLASS BRAID (STRENGTH AND SUPPORT)

SILICONE JACKET (RESISTANT TO HEAT, MOISTURE, CHEMICALS, OIL, OZONE)

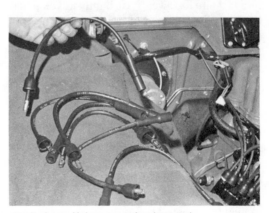

GOOD REPLACEMENT CABLES are well made (left)—and they aren't cheap. Unless severely mistreated, however, their long life can make them worth their cost. A custom-made replacement set (right) comes cut to length. They will already be assembled and ready for installation on your car.

boot back along the cable a bit to expose the terminal, although the boot should fit snugly. It won't slide along the cable as though greased. Original-equipment cables—and some replacements—have boots molded in place at the cable ends. Don't try to break this bond.

Clean the distributor cap

If a cable shows evidence of arcing at the distributor-cap end, remove the distributor cap and clean deposits from each socket with a distributor-cap cleaning tool. Clean the coil tower. Deposits increase resistance.

The visual inspection shows clearly if cables are cracked and also lets you check the condition of terminals. You can also "probe" the cables to reveal small punctures that might go unnoticed. To make the problem test, get a jumper wire with an alligator clip at each end. Clip one end to a clean ground on the engine and the other to the shank of a screwdriver.

Start the engine and let it idle. Remove one cable from the sparkplug. Be sure that the boot end of the cable is positioned so it doesn't point to a ground. Probe all around cable and its boot. If a puncture is present, a spark will jump from the defective area to the probe. Discard the cable.

To test the high-tension cable between the center tower of the distributor and the coil tower, keep the cable connected, but be sure to disconnect one sparkplug cable.

If cables pass your tests, reconnect them. To install cables into distributor towers enter each terminal into its tower. Push lightly as you pinch the large diameter part of the boot to release air trapped between the boot and tower. Continue pushing until the cable is firmly seated.

Before seating cables on sparkplugs, wipe off sparkplug insulators. All connections must be secure to avoid arcing.

One more possibility

Even though cables pass all tests up to this point, they may still be the cause of misfire. A cable that looks perfectly sound can be damaged internally. Internal damage is caused primarily by manhandling. When a cable is pulled, the inner core can break. This increases resistance,

reducing current to the sparkplug.

If you have an ohmmeter, you can find out if cables are damaged internally by testing resistance. Do one cable at a time, as follows (this test assumes that your car is equipped with electronic suppression cable, identified by marks on it):

1. Disconnect the cable from the sparkplug and attach a sparkplug adapter between the cable and sparkplug if your ohmmeter lead has an alligator clip.

2. Remove the distributor cap, but keep cables connected.

3. Connect ohmmeter between sparkplug adapter and the correct electrode inside distributor cap for the cable you are testing. If ohmmeter leads are probe types, you can disconnect the cable from the plug and insert the probe so it touches the terminal. Check that probes make good contact.

4. If resistance is more than 30,000 ohms for cables up to 25 inches long and 50,000 ohms for cables longer than 25 inches, remove the cable from the tower and check its resistance by probing the terminal. Replace cables that fail to meet the 30,000- or 50,000-ohm specifications.

5. If a cable meets specification when disconnected but flunks when hooked to the distributor, a problem exists in the distributor cap. Clean out deposits from inside the cap and test again.

6. To test the cable between the coil and distributor cap, connect the ohmmeter between the center contact in the cap and either primary terminal at the coil. Combined resistance should not exceed 25,000 ohms. If it does, remove the cable at the coil and test resistance. If it is more than 15,000 ohms, replace the cable. If less, check for a loose connection at the tower and for a faulty coil.

The best replacement high-tension cables are expensive, but worth it. The latest design uses tough silicone rubber for the core, jacket and even boots. It is by far the sturdiest and longest lasting cable yet made. You should get an easy 50,000 miles of service unless you start playing tug-of-war.

Most cable makers offer sets as "custom" or "universal." A "custom" set is designed for a specific engine; a "universal" set for several engines.

Read your sparkplugs

■ ARE YOU SPARKPLUG smart? See if you can answer these questions:
● What has gone wrong when the top part of a sparkplug insulator shows vertical black streaks?
● What's the problem when a sparkplug's center electrode shows burning and extreme wear?
● What is corona, when is it most likely to occur and what should be done about it?

Here are the answers:

1. The plug was improperly installed. In all likelihood, it was overtightened or an open-end wrench was used that distorted the shell, which led to the blowby that caused the streaks.

2. This condition is usually caused by improperly compressed or corroded gaskets which had been tightened down onto dirty seats. The normal flow of heat away from the sparkplug was prevented, resulting in overheating.

3. Corona is a high-voltage electric phenomenon that makes sparkplugs and sparkplug cables glow. It most often occurs in damp weather and is especially visible in the dark. Nothing has to be done about it.

Sparkplug—that's an electrical component used in a gasoline engine's ignition system to provide a high-tension-voltage spark for igniting the fuel mixture.

When new plugs are needed

No one can argue with the fact that worn sparkplugs are a chief cause of hard starting, poor engine performance and increased fuel use.

Sparkplug performance is the most important single factor in maintaining your gasoline mileage and engine efficiency. Tests show that if only one sparkplug out of eight is misfiring, gasoline mileage may fall off as much as 15.2 percent.

However, sparkplugs are frequently blamed for poor engine performance which they don't cause. The story of a car owner who installs a set of new sparkplugs to cure engine misfiring and power loss is typical.

The remedy works, but only for a few hundred miles. What's happened is that the new plugs temporarily improve engine performance, because new plugs make less of a demand on the ignition system.

But new sparkplugs cannot permanently rectify poor engine performance that is being caused by worn distributor contact points, cracked distributor cap, unspecified ignition timing or a weak coil. Or for that matter, by worn rings or cylinders, or faulty carburetion.

The best way to tell if sparkplugs are to blame for your problem is to examine them carefully

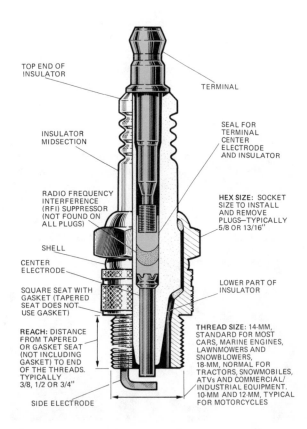

TOP END OF INSULATOR

TERMINAL

INSULATOR MIDSECTION

SEAL FOR TERMINAL CENTER ELECTRODE AND INSULATOR

RADIO FREQUENCY INTERFERENCE (RFI) SUPPRESSOR (NOT FOUND ON ALL PLUGS)

HEX SIZE: SOCKET SIZE TO INSTALL AND REMOVE PLUGS—TYPICALLY 5/8 OR 13/16"

SHELL

CENTER ELECTRODE

SQUARE SEAT WITH GASKET (TAPERED SEAT DOES NOT USE GASKET)

LOWER PART OF INSULATOR

REACH: DISTANCE FROM TAPERED OR GASKET SEAT (NOT INCLUDING GASKET) TO END OF THE THREADS. TYPICALLY 3/8, 1/2 OR 3/4"

THREAD SIZE: 14-MM, STANDARD FOR MOST CARS, MARINE ENGINES, LAWNMOWERS AND SNOWBLOWERS, 18-MM, NORMAL FOR TRACTORS, SNOWMOBILES, ATVs AND COMMERCIAL/ INDUSTRIAL EQUIPMENT. 10-MM AND 12-MM, TYPICAL FOR MOTORCYCLES

SIDE ELECTRODE

WHY SPARKPLUGS MISFIRE

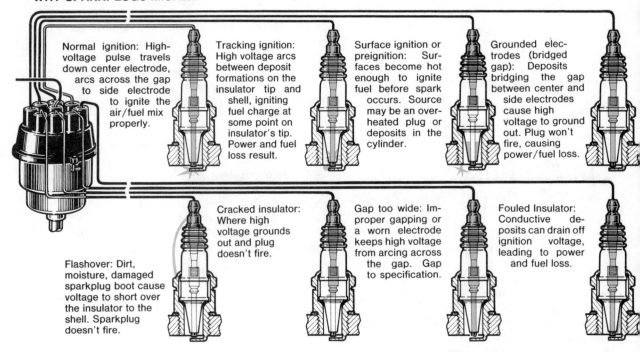

Normal ignition: High-voltage pulse travels down center electrode, arcs across the gap to side electrode to ignite the air/fuel mix properly.

Tracking ignition: High voltage arcs between deposit formations on the insulator tip and shell, igniting fuel charge at some point on insulator's tip. Power and fuel loss result.

Surface ignition or preignition: Surfaces become hot enough to ignite fuel before spark occurs. Source may be an overheated plug or deposits in the cylinder.

Grounded electrodes (bridged gap): Deposits bridging the gap between center and side electrodes cause high voltage to ground out. Plug won't fire, causing power/fuel loss.

Flashover: Dirt, moisture, damaged sparkplug boot cause voltage to short over the insulator to the shell. Sparkplug doesn't fire.

Cracked insulator: Where high voltage grounds out and plug doesn't fire.

Gap too wide: Improper gapping or a worn electrode keeps high voltage from arcing across the gap. Gap to specification.

Fouled Insulator: Conductive deposits can drain off ignition voltage, leading to power and fuel loss.

when you take them from the engine. Look for conditions shown in the photos. If one exists, then a sparkplug or plugs are causing trouble.

You should also analyze the tips of used sparkplugs carefully. They can provide clues to what's happening in the engine and to the plugs themselves.

Removing plugs correctly

In most cases, the tools you need are a ¹³⁄₁₆-in. hex or ⅝-in. hex sparkplug socket, a ratchet wrench and an extension.

You can find out the hex size you need by checking service data in a manual or asking a dealer selling your make of car.

Don't confuse hex size with two other sparkplug dimensions—thread size and reach. The lead illustration has an explanation of all three.

In some cases, "conventional" tools won't do. Where quarters are too close to get a wrench and extension onto a plug, use a flexible sparkplug wrench. It consists of a socket on the end of a flexible hose-type extension with a T-bar handle, sold where auto tools are sold.

SPARKPLUGS are cleaned by inserting tip into a sandblasting machine.

FILING ELECTRODES may be necessary to remove stubborn deposits.

CLEANING THREADS is important to insure proper seating of plug in block.

HOW TO TIGHTEN SPARKPLUGS

PLUG SIZE	WITH TORQUE WRENCH (ft.-lbs.)		WITHOUT TORQUE WRENCH
	Cast Iron Head	Aluminum Head	Cast Iron or Aluminum Head
10 mm	8-12	8-12	⅜ to ½ turn
12 mm	10-18	10-18	¼ turn
14 mm, gasket seat	25-30	18-22	½ to ¾ turn
14 mm, tapered seat	7-15	7-15	*.
18 mm, gasket seat	32-38	28-34	½ to ¾ turn
18 mm, tapered seat	15-20	15-20	*

*Champion suggests that tapered-seat sparkplugs be turned 1/32 to 1/16 turn beyond finger tight.

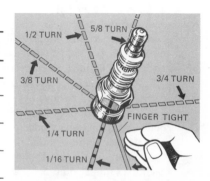

THE ART of tightening plugs without a torque wrench is aided by diagram.

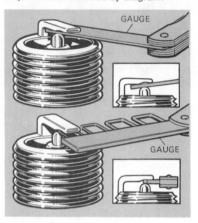

OLD DESIGN   NEW DESIGN

TWO TYPES of plugs for rotary engines use two outer electrodes.

FLAT FEELER gauge won't give an accurate reading; use the round wire type.

The following procedure is the conventional, correct way to remove sparkplugs from an engine:

1. *Mark each sparkplug cable* with some identifying symbol so it can be reinstalled in its correct cylinder. Accidentally switching cables leads to plugs firing out of sequence, which can cause serious engine damage.

One method you can use to mark cables is to attach a clip-type clothespin or masking tape marked with a number to each cable as you remove it. The numbering system you use in the case of a V8 engine may be R-1, R-2, R-3 and R-4 for plug cables on the right (passenger) side of the car, and L-1, L-2, L-3 and L-4 for plug cables on the left (driver) side.

2. *Rotate the sparkplug boot* about one-quarter turn while pulling it off.

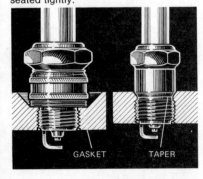

GASKET ON plug at left should be seated tightly.

GASKET   TAPER

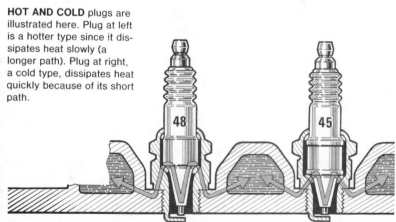

HOT AND COLD plugs are illustrated here. Plug at left is a hotter type since it dissipates heat slowly (a longer path). Plug at right, a cold type, dissipates heat quickly because of its short path.

Caution: Never pull on the sparkplug cable itself. Rough handling will cause separation of the conductive strands, which will lead to an open circuit, poor conductivity, excessive resistance and sparkplug misfire. Pull only on the boot.

3. *Loosen each sparkplug* one turn only after cables have been removed.

Caution: Aluminum-head engines must be cool before removing plugs since plugs in a warm engine will seize and be difficult to unscrew.

4. *Blow away carbon and dirt* from around each sparkplug. Compressed air is best to use, but if an air hose isn't available use a length of vacuum hose. Aim one end at the area and blow through the other.

5. *Remove each plug* and place it in its appropriate hole in a sparkplug tray that is numbered to coincide with the number of cylinders in your car. Proper identification is important so you can relate the particular plug with the cylinder to make a proper diagnosis of sparkplug condition.

Service tip: If a sparkplug is difficult to remove, unscrew it slightly to expose a few threads. Drip some light oil on the threads and screw the plug back into place. Let oil soak the threads before you try removing the plug again.

Servicing plugs

It is extravagant to throw away a set of plugs that can be cleaned, adjusted and put back in service. However, to do a thorough job of cleaning use a sparkplug cleaner.

Where do you get a sparkplug cleaner? You can buy one made for home garage use. If you don't care to do this, take the plugs to a local service station and pay them to do the job for you.

To service plugs correctly, proceed as follows:

1. *Wipe the plug clean* to remove moisture, oil and dirt.

2. *If the firing end* of a plug is oily or coated with wet deposits, wash the plug in a cleaning solvent, such as kerosene. Use a brush to work solvent into the lower insulator cavity. Dry the plug with compressed air—even if you have to beg an air hose. If the tip of a freshly washed plug isn't dried thoroughly, the cleaning solvent can cake deep within the plug and hinder plug performance.

3. *Clean plugs* in the cleaning machine.

Caution: Don't blast a plug for more than five seconds. Longer application could wear down the insulator and electrodes.

4. *Open the outside electrode* enough to slip a sparkplug file between electrodes. Use the gap adjusting tool of a sparkplug feeler gauge tool. Do not use pliers or any tool except a sparkplug

tool to spread the electrode. If you do, irreparable damage may be done to the plug.

5. *File the center* and outside electrodes clean. Only one or two passes are necessary. Filing is important since the cleaning machine doesn't always remove electrode scale.

6. *Examine threads closely* for carbon and scale that could keep a sparkplug from seating itself properly. Clean threads with a small hand or machine-powered wire brush.

Important: Be careful that you don't touch electrodes with the brush. You may damage them.

7. *Use a sparkplug wire-type feeler gauge* to gap plugs. A flat feeler gauge of the type used to adjust distributor breaker points will give an erroneous adjustment. Use the gap adjusting tool to set gap by bending the side electrode.

Caution: Do *not* bend the center electrode. If you do, you will have to discard the sparkplug.

Set gap to the exact specification in your manual or to that shown on the servicing decal in the engine compartment of your car. Gap is set properly when you feel a slight amount of friction as you move the feeler gauge back and forth between electrodes.

Important: Whether you are installing reconditioned or new sparkplugs, the gap of each one you put into your car's engine must be set before installation.

Installing plugs

If your engine has an aluminum head, apply a *thin* coat of graphite grease to the first two or three threads of each sparkplug. This helps prevent seizing.

Clean the cylinder head threads with a thread chaser, which you can buy in an auto-parts store, or with a small brush. If plugs use gaskets and are being put back in service, replace the old gaskets with new ones. Seat the gasket fully by threading it on so it fits flush against the base of the shell.

Tapered seat sparkplugs do not use gaskets.

If your engine uses tapered seat sparkplugs, it cannot use sparkplugs with gaskets. If your engine uses sparkplugs with gaskets, it cannot use tapered seat sparkplugs.

Screw the sparkplugs finger tight into the cylinder head and stop. Here is where we come to an impasse.

Most leading companies recommend the use of a torque wrench to tighten sparkplugs. Some, on the other hand, contend that practically no one uses a torque wrench on sparkplugs, and it is not really required.

What do *you* do? If you have (or can borrow) a

torque wrench, use it. If you don't, use the "feel" method.

In either event, sparkplugs must be tightened *exactly* to the specifications given here which have been devised by the International Standards Organization and Society of Automotive Engineers. Although plugs won't seem to be tight, they will be tight enough. If you take liberties with these specifications, you will overtighten the plugs.

Caution: Be very careful that you don't cross-thread plugs when putting them into the cylinder head. You could ruin the threads of sparkplug ports.

Selecting sparkplugs

This should cause you no problem. You start by choosing the sparkplug recommended for your engine by the car's manufacturer. This recommendation is in the owner's manual and on the service decal in the engine compartment.

We aren't going to discuss the numbering systems of sparkplugs here. It's interesting, but irrelevant since each sparkplug manufacturer has devised his own. All we want to do is emphasize that you start with the number that your car's manufacturer says to use.

Now, if this plug doesn't operate satisfactorily for the driving conditions you encounter, a plug that is colder or hotter in the heat range may be substituted. The heat range of a sparkplug is determined primarily by the length of the lower insulator. The longer the insulator is, the hotter the plug will operate. The shorter the insulator is, the colder the plug will operate.

There are three rules to follow in selecting the exact heat range plug that will operate best in your engine:

1. Select sparkplugs having the heat range specified by the car's manufacturer.

2. If plugs overheat (lower insulator blisters or turns ghostly white, and/or electrodes wear prematurely), switch to sparkplugs of the *same* make of the next lower (colder) heat range.

3. If plugs foul (firing tips get oily or sooty), switch to sparkplugs of the *same* make of the next higher (hotter) heat range.

Suppression vs. non-suppression

Automotive electrical systems have long been recognized as a major source of radio frequency interference (RFI). With almost 150 million cars, trucks and buses on the road, there's a lot of radio and TV interference. To keep it in harness, all vehicles are equipped with suppression devices at the factory.

As far as cars are concerned, these suppression devices take the form of so-called resistor sparkplugs, suppressor-type secondary cables or external suppressors. Frequently, resistor sparkplugs are combined with suppressor cables or external suppressors. Suppressor cables and external suppressors are not recommended for combined use.

Regarding the selection of sparkplugs, if the manufacturer's original equipment calls for resistor-type sparkplugs, then it is suggested that you use them.

SPARKPLUGS THAT INDICATE NORMAL ENGINE OPERATION

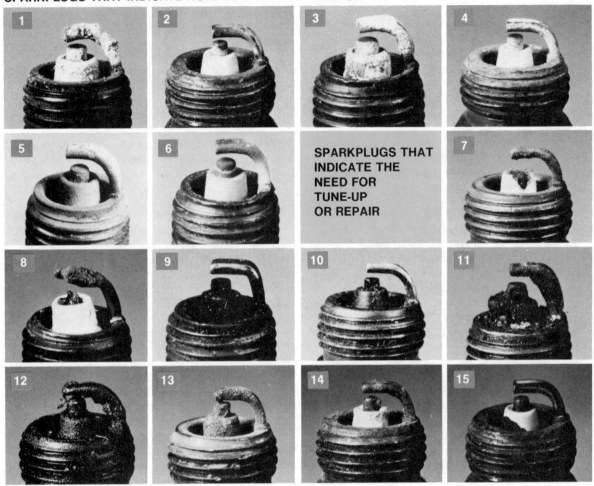

SPARKPLUGS THAT INDICATE THE NEED FOR TUNE-UP OR REPAIR

In the photos above are sparkplugs taken from 15 different engines. Here's how to "read" them.

1. Almost white, fluffy gray deposit on insulator tip and side electrode is normal for emission-controlled engines using lean mixtures and no-lead fuels. This plug has high mileage and should be replaced.

2. White with light tan tint: The soft deposits on center electrode and darker deposit on side electrode indicate proper heat range for the way this engine is being used—at moderate speeds and loads.

3. Light tan deposits on a well-used plug: The yellow deposit on the side electrode is normal and comes from metallic additives.

4. Yellowish, soft white deposits on the center electrode and insulator are normal for an engine using fuel containing certain metallic additives. Deposits on the shell are normal and show no signs of over-rich or over-lean fuel mixtures.

5. Classic example of a normal plug with fluffy, chocolate brown deposit on the insulator. Note slightly lighter color on side electrode showing that it's running a bit hotter. Sooty black deposit on shell suggests rich mixture, perhaps need for new air filter.

6. Fluffy red deposits are normal in engines using fuels with MMT additives. Slightly oily deposit on the shell may be due to an engine not yet fully broken in. In an older engine it might indicate the beginning of wear on piston rings, valve guides/seals.

Problem sparkplugs 7 through 15:

7. Detonation damage: The firing end of the insulator is broken and metal transferred from center electrode to the side electrode. Possible causes: a. Overadvanced ignition timing. b. Fuel too low in octane. c. EGR system malfunctioning.

8. Preignition damage. White deposits on a blistered insulator, along with burned electrodes, reveal extreme heat condition. Possible causes: a. Sparkplug too hot. b. Overadvanced ignition timing. c. Glowing deposits in combustion chamber. d. Cooling system clogged. e. Exhaust system blocked.

9. Soot fouling. Fluffy, black soot deposits on insulator and electrodes. Possible causes: a. Excessively rich mixture due to sticking choke or defective carburetor. b. Faulty ignition primary circuit or defective sparkplug wires. c. Excessively cold starting without engine warm-up.

10. Oil fouled. Oily, usually black deposit covering insulator and electrodes. Possi-

ble causes: a. Excessive passage of engine oil into combustion chamber due to piston ring or valve guide seal leakage. b. Defective PCV system.

11. Carbon fouled. Hard, black carbon deposits on insulator and electrodes. Possible causes: a. Moderate amount of oil passing rings or valves. b. Defective PCV system. c. Sparkplug too cold. d. Sparkplug not correct type for engine.

12. Dirt fouling. Carbonized and sometimes granular deposits on and around the insulator and electrodes. Possible causes: a. Air cleaner missing. b. Defective air-cleaner mountings.

13. Bridged gap. Carbon particles are lodged in the sparkplug gap. Possible cause: Combustion chamber deposits accumulated during low-speed, light-load use break loose during demand for full power.

14. Glazed insulator. Glassy surface on the insulator as a result of deposits melting on plug. Possible causes: a. Sparkplug too hot. b. Local overheating due to cooling system-blockage or similar defect.

15. Splashed insulator. Splotches of black, almost paint-like deposits on the insulator. Possible causes: Delayed correction of an engine miss allows soft, oily deposits to accumulate in cylinder. After tune-up these deposits break loose and foul plug.

Patio bug control

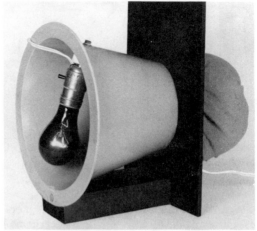

WHEN MOSQUITOES flock to the light bulb, the fan immediately sucks them into the trap for later disposal.

■ SITTING ON AN OPEN patio during a cool summer evening sounds great, but how many times have you been chased inside by mosquitoes and other nighttime insects? The hanging bug trap you see here solved one patio bug problem for good.

Black light attracts most insects. Place a 100-w. black-light bulb in a plastic flowerpot after cutting a hole in the bottom. Using the pot as a funnel, fasten it over a same-size hole in a piece of plywood, then bolt a small electric suction fan (4½ in. sq.) to the back to suck the insects from the bulb into a bag made from pantyhose. Once drawn in the trap, the bugs can't escape back through the fan—it works like a charm.

Attach the fan to the back of the plywood with four small stovebolts. The drain hole in the bottom of the plastic pot can be enlarged to 2 in. or so with a round file, leaving a flange around the inside for attaching the pot to the plywood with two small bolts. A short ⅛-in. pipe nipple and nut holds the socket to the pot.

Make the trap from discarded pantyhose by cutting off the legs as shown below and tying the ends in a square knot. The elastic top of the hose grips the fan snugly.

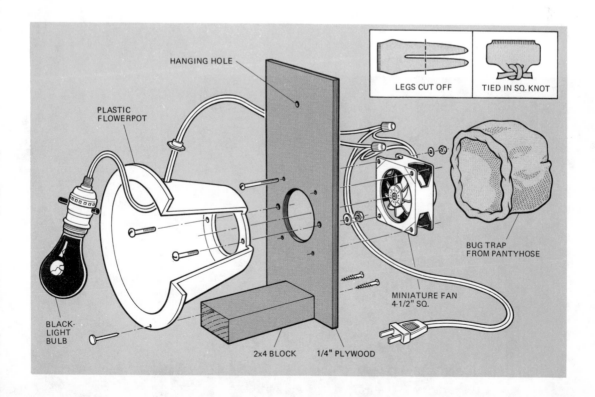

HANGING HOLE

LEGS CUT OFF

TIED IN SQ. KNOT

PLASTIC FLOWERPOT

BUG TRAP FROM PANTYHOSE

MINIATURE FAN 4-1/2" SQ.

BLACK-LIGHT BULB

2x4 BLOCK

1/4" PLYWOOD

Termite control

1. ANTENNA
STRAIGHT
BEADLIKE

TERMITE

2. THORAX AND
ABDOMEN
BROADLY JOINED

■ WHAT'S THE USUAL reaction when a homeowner discovers termites in his house? Sheer panic.

Actually the discovery of termites is *not* an occasion for panic because time is on the homeowner's side. Even a mature, well established colony of 60,000 workers eats only ⅕ ounce of wood a day. There's plenty of time to approach the problem rationally and get bids on a termite control job.

Most Americans need worry about only two types of termites. The drywood termite is important mainly to homeowners along the southern rim of the United States, especially in Florida, California and Hawaii. Where they do occur, drywood termites post a serious problem because they need no contact with the soil. They can enter the house under shingles, through cracks in windows and eaves or through screened vents in the attic, and if they become well established, the house must be fumigated.

TERMITES AT WORK—here they are nibbling away in one of the galleries they love to create.

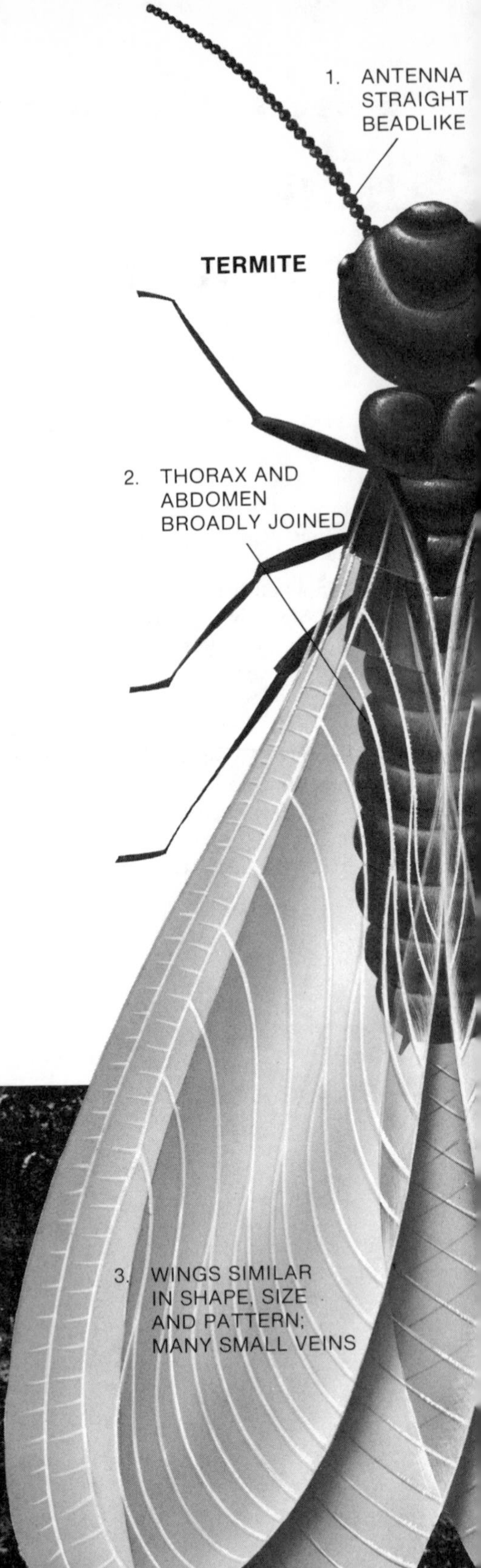

3. WINGS SIMILAR
IN SHAPE, SIZE
AND PATTERN;
MANY SMALL VEINS

1. ANTENNA
   "ELBOWED"

ANT

2. THORAX AND
   ABDOMEN JOINED
   BY A NARROW WAIST

3. WINGS NOT
   ALIKE IN SHAPE
   SIZE OR PATTERN;
   FEW VEINS

The subterranean termite is more common. Found in every state except Alaska, this one must have warm air and moisture. To stay moist, it builds tubes made of soil as it goes. Of course it won't need to build tubes if wood is already touching the soil. Cut off its contact with moisture, whether it's direct contact with soil or through mud tubes, and you can solve practically any termite problem.

The eight major danger areas for termite entry are:

■ *Cracks in concrete.* Because termites eat only wood, people have a false sense of security about concrete-slab foundations. They don't realize that slabs often develop cracks that allow termites hidden access to the house framing. Wood posts provide an access route when the post goes all the way through the concrete and contacts soil underneath. For protection, the soil beneath slabs and footings should be treated with a termite insecticide.

■ *Earth fill under porches.* Here, again, concrete may give false security. If the concrete porch has earth fill underneath it, soil may be in contact with framing members. To be safe, make certain soil is at least 8 in. below the lowest wooden member.

CRACK IN concrete slab (below left) can give termites an entry into your house.

SCRAP LUMBER in earth-floored basement (below) invites termite infestation.

TERMITES, with access to wood from soil that is completely unchecked, can do this kind of damage.

RAIL-SUPPORT POSTS in contact with soil provide another excellent opportunity for termites.

■ *Buried wood.* Too often, wood scraps left over from construction are buried near the house or forms are left in place after pouring the foundation.

■ *Leaking pipes and faucets.* These can provide all the moisture needed for a thriving termite colony. The same holds true for gutter downspouts that fail to carry water away from the building.

■ *Poor ventilation.* When air doesn't circulate, moisture forms. This is a special hazard in crawlspaces, so adequate venting should be installed to assure good cross-ventilation. Be sure that shrubbery doesn't block vent openings.

■ *Flower planters.* Planters built near the house should be waterproofed below soil level. An air space between planter and house is an added safeguard.

■ *Porch steps.* If in contact with soil, wood porch steps offer termites their own stairway to your home. Steps should rest on a concrete apron and soil below should be protected.

■ *Wood trellises.* A common mistake—often after taking other precautions against termites—is to build a wood trellis that provides a direct link from soil to house.

The best time to think about termites, of course, is *before* your house or addition is built. It's easy—just make certain that your builder's contract calls for soil pretreatment with a termite insecticide.

Soil pretreatment includes spraying of all the soil that will be underneath or around the outside edge of the house with a chemical. It's done after the foundation footing trenches, plumbing and electrical conduits are in place—just before laying the vapor barrier and pouring the slab. Extra chemicals should be poured in those areas adjacent to foundation walls and interior walls, and around sewer and utility openings. When buying a termite-control job for an existing house, be sure to check the operator's references.

Jewelry you can carve

■ THESE MINIATURES can be carved, from start to finish, on a kitchen table, so you won't need a king-sized workshop for the project. And the nature of the job requires just a small amount of material—even scraps which you probably have on hand can be used. Further, the tools that make it all possible are available at reasonable cost.

Mini carving is a wise choice for beginners.

Unlike sculpture, you needn't be either an artist or an advanced craftsman to try your hand at it. As can be seen in the step-by-step photos showing the creation of an elephant in the round, a minimum number of steps is required. Because of their small size, any errors or imperfections will be virtually invisible. Ideas are easy to come by; encyclopedias, magazines and books are excellent sources for inspiration.

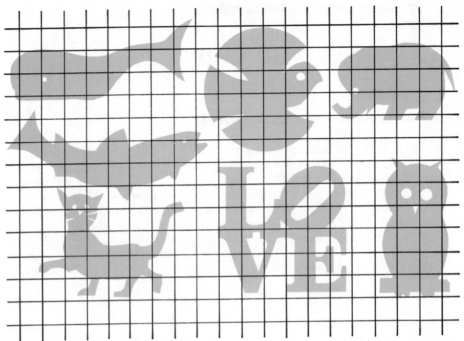

SOME OF THE articles shown were made using the patterns shown above. Using the square grid, you can adjust the size to fit your needs.

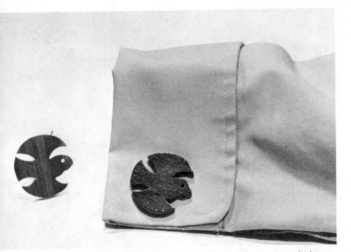

CUFF LINKS were "carved" on a jigsaw, sanded smooth, then glued to jewelry hardware.

Carving in the flat

Actually, some of these pieces are not carvings at all. Letters, the peace dove and the like are simply drawn on a piece of wood from ⅛ to 3/16 in. thick and then cut out on a jigsaw. The edges are then sanded and buffed to a smooth finish and the carving can be put to use as a pendant, pin or tie tack. For a hanging piece, such as the pendant, simply drill a hole and use a rawhide thong as the "necklace." Or you can fashion a hanger mount as shown in the drawing. This is then glued in a predrilled hole with an adhesive such as super glue. The appropriate finding loop is then attached.

Flat carvings can be cut from wood or plastic or a combination of the two. When cutting acrylic plastic with a jigsaw, use a 14-tooth blade. (A finer blade causes heat which welds the plastic behind the saw cut.)

To glue veneer to plastic or plastic to plastic, apply cement liberally to the surfaces to be joined and clamp the piece overnight between two pieces of wood. Make certain the wood is separated from the workpiece with wax paper because glue oozes out as the clamp pressure is increased.

Next day, remove the hardened excess glue using a sharp knife. The flat is now ready to saw to shape. After sawing, sand and buff the edges

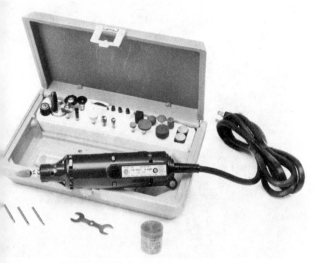

BASIC TOOL used for the carvings comes in a 34-piece kit including wrench. Tungsten carbide bits are extras.

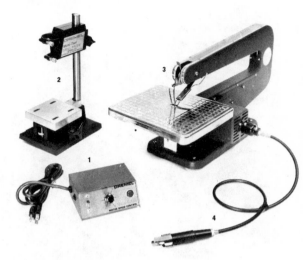

OTHER TOOLS that will speed work: 1. variable-speed control; 2. drill-press accessory; 3. hobbyist's jigsaw; 4. flexible shaft (used with jigsaw).

MATERIALS used: 1. jewelry findings (cuff links, earrings, tie-tack shown); 2. plexiglass; 3. veneers, solid wood; and, 4. glue to affix carvings to hardware.

CARVINGS shown above are examples of plastic glued to plastic (top), wood to plastic, and plastic glued over veneer.

smooth. Drill the hole for the hanger if the carving is to be a necklace or simply glue the carving to the appropriate jewelry hardware. For a hand-rubbed look, a clear plastic coating, the type which comes in an aerosol container, works best. Three light coats are better than one thick one. It is also best to spray flat pieces with them lying down rather than suspended—when the first side is dry, flop the piece and spray the second side.

Carving in the round

Though three-dimensional carving is slightly more difficult than flat carving, it is also more satisfying. For these carvings, use thicker stock—5/16 to 3/8 in. Steps for carving in the round are shown in the photos. After cutting out the shape, use the powered carver and various cutters to begin rough shaping to give the piece form in the third dimension.

TRANSFER the design from grid paper to a wood block using carbon paper beneath the drawing. Tape the carbon and drawing so they can't shift.

CUT THE figure out with the jigsaw. The stock for the elephant is cherry, 5/16 in. thick. Using the blade guard helps you reduce chatter.

MOUNT THE carving tool in the drill press accessory and drill the eyehole first. Unlike large presses, this one's head remains stationary. The work table is raised to the drill with the knob.

CARVING starts with knurled cutter. The shop-built jig facilitates handling the small piece. Jig (below) is gripped in a vise.

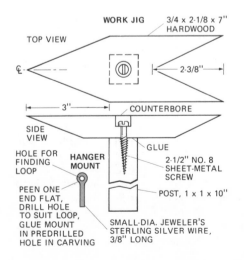

WORK JIG 3/4 x 2-1/8 x 7" HARDWOOD

TOP VIEW

2-3/8"

3" COUNTERBORE

SIDE VIEW

HOLE FOR FINDING LOOP

HANGER MOUNT

GLUE

2-1/2" NO. 8 SHEET-METAL SCREW

POST, 1 x 1 x 10"

PEEN ONE END FLAT, DRILL HOLE TO SUIT LOOP, GLUE MOUNT IN PREDRILLED HOLE IN CARVING

SMALL-DIA. JEWELER'S STERLING SILVER WIRE, 3/8" LONG

AFTER ROUGH shaping, grind the carving smooth with an emery-point dressing wheel. Since the form is hand-held, power carving calls for extra care.

THE FINISHED gift from the workbench is ready for gift-wrapping. For looks, line the box with black velvet around a card or tissue as shown.

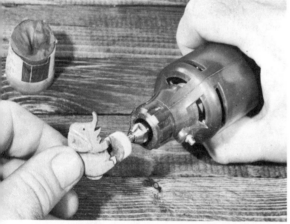

TO FINISH, the carving is polished with buffing rouge and a cloth pad chucked in the tool. The pad is recharged by dipping it in the rouge.

Keep in mind that the tool's cutter rotates at 30,000 rpm. And since the carving is small, and fingertip-held, care should be taken to keep fingers clear of the cutter's path. Never start a cut from the end and work toward the middle; always start a cut in a "meat" portion of the wood and progress shaping toward an end. If you start a cut at the end grain, the tool may jump in the opposite direction. Also, don't try to cut away too much wood in one pass. A series of light passes is easier to control and permits more graceful shaping.

Final finishing

With the piece roughed out, start smoothing using a grinder. For this step, using the variable-speed control, adjust the tool speed to lower rpm. High rpm will leave burn marks on wood and plastic. To sand hard-to-get-at spots, trim an emery board to a point. When satisfied with the smoothness, spray the piece with a clear plastic coating. When completely dry, polish the piece with the buffing wheel and polishing rouge as shown.

These mini carvings make excellent gifts for Christmas or birthday giving. The ideas shown here are just some of many possibilities. Use your imagination. Try making a peace pendant or dove for a teenager, a lapel pin for your wife, or a fish tie-tack for any anglers you know. To give the carvings that expensive jewelry look for gift giving, wrap them in boxes lined with black velvet.

Jewelry box fit for a queen

■ SURPRISINGLY, this jewelry box is a lot easier to build than a first look may imply. It features a case veneered on all sides and a single-tune musical movement which plays when the lid is opened. Though veneering requires care and accurate cutting, none of the steps is particularly difficult if you take your time.

• *Panels.* Cut all veneer blanks slightly oversize. And, since it is brittle, the face of thuya, or any fragile crotch or burl veneer, should be taped (masking or kraft) near all edges and across any cracks before you cut it with a knife or veneer saw. Apply white glue liberally to the veneer (remember, keep the taped side outside) and affix the veneer to hardboard. Clamp this between waxed paper and cauls and, applying pressure slowly, work from the center out.

Trim the oversize veneer blanks to remove loose veneer and excess glue from edges, peel off tape and rough-sand the veneer to remove all glue that has seeped through. Finish the blanks by trimming to dimensions shown in the drawing.

Cut oversize backing panels from plywood and glue them to the back of each veneered panel. Trim the plywood panels flush with veneered panels on all sides, except the ends of the back panel which are trimmed 1/16 in. oversize to fit the grooves in the rear corner posts.

• *Drawers.* Cut three blanks for drawer fronts from ¼-in. hardboard and veneer them with thuya. After rough-sanding the veneered blanks, trim two of them for drawers and the third for the false drawer. Glue rosewood veneer to all four edges of the two drawer fronts and sand these to size. Now remove ¼ in. of thuya from all four sides of the three drawer fronts with a sharp chisel and glue the inlay borders in place. Locate knob screw holes, stack and clamp the drawer fronts and drill the holes.

Drawer parts are of ¼-in. mahogany and ⅛-

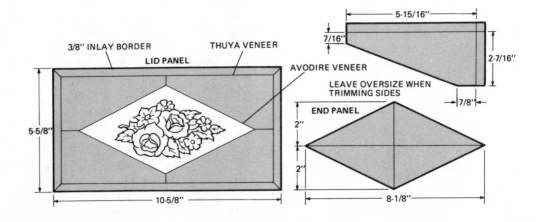

3/8" INLAY BORDER   THUYA VENEER

LID PANEL

5-5/8"

10-5/8"

AVODIRE VENEER

LEAVE OVERSIZE WHEN TRIMMING SIDES

END PANEL

2"

2"

8-1/8"

5-15/16"

7/16"

2-7/16"

7/8"

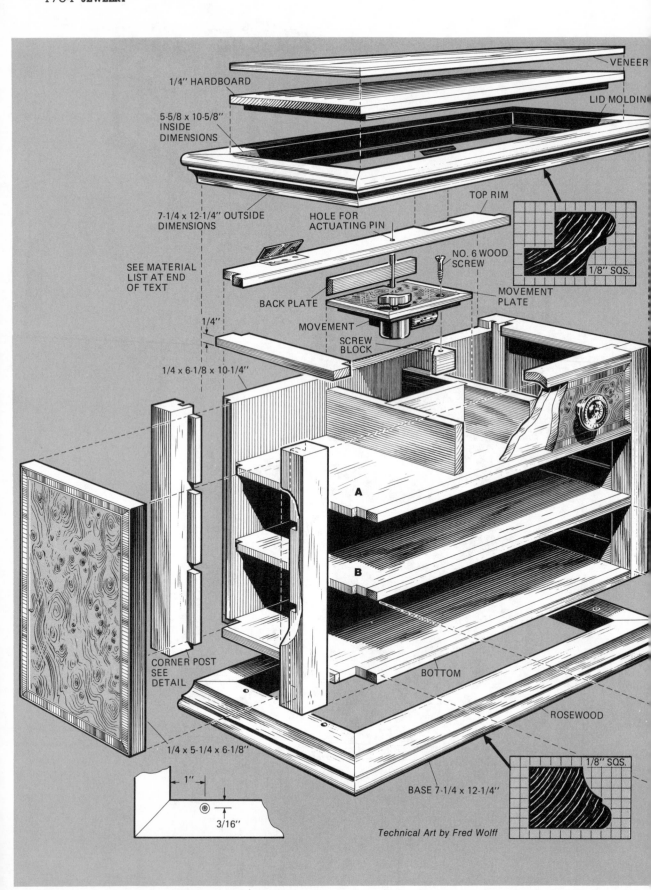

VENEER

1/4" HARDBOARD

LID MOLDING

5-5/8 x 10-5/8"
INSIDE
DIMENSIONS

7-1/4 x 12-1/4" OUTSIDE
DIMENSIONS

HOLE FOR
ACTUATING PIN

TOP RIM

SEE MATERIAL
LIST AT END
OF TEXT

NO. 6 WOOD
SCREW

1/8" SQS.

BACK PLATE

MOVEMENT
PLATE

1/4"

MOVEMENT

1/4 x 6-1/8 x 10-1/4"

SCREW
BLOCK

A

B

CORNER POST
SEE
DETAIL

BOTTOM

1/4 x 5-1/4 x 6-1/8"

ROSEWOOD

1"

3/16"

BASE 7-1/4 x 12-1/4"

1/8" SQS.

Technical Art by Fred Wolff

in. plywood. Glue drawer fronts to the drawers with the bottom edges flush. Redrill the knob screw holes and countersink them on the inside (later a layer of velveteen will cover the screw-heads).

• *Lid and base.* Select the portion of floral inlay to be used and carefully trim away mahogany background and unwanted portions with a sharp chisel. Then, lay out the pattern for the avodire diamond shape on white paper. Center the floral inlay and trace the outline with a sharp pencil. Cut avodire veneer and two pieces of scrap

veneer and glue the pattern to one piece of the scrap veneer. Sandwich the avodire veneer between the scrap pieces and tape the edges securely.

With a fine blade in your scroll saw, cut out the floral pattern and taped veneers together. After you cut to the outside of the diamond pattern, carefully separate the avodire veneer from scrap.

• *Movement.* A little trial-and-error fitting is in order here. Before cutting blanks or drilling any holes, refer to the movement that you have on hand and determine dimensions from it. (They

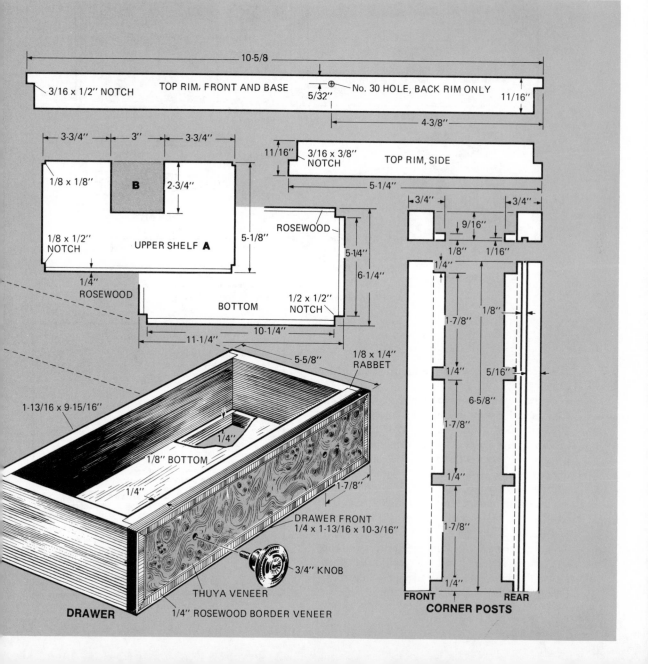

DRAWER

CORNER POSTS

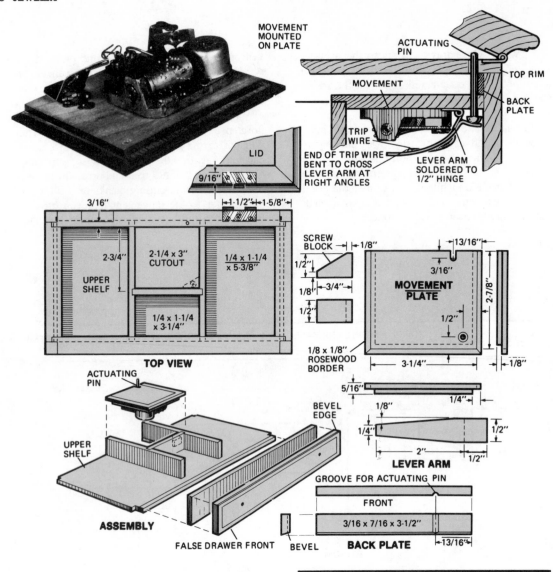

MOVEMENT
MOUNTED
ON PLATE

ACTUATING
PIN

MOVEMENT

TOP RIM

BACK
PLATE

TRIP
WIRE

END OF TRIP WIRE
BENT TO CROSS
LEVER ARM AT
RIGHT ANGLES

LEVER ARM
SOLDERED TO
1/2" HINGE

LID

9/16"

3/16"

1-1/2" 1-5/8"

2-3/4"

2-1/4 x 3"
CUTOUT

1/4 x 1-1/4
x 5-3/8"

UPPER
SHELF

1/4 x 1-1/4
x 3-1/4"

TOP VIEW

SCREW
BLOCK

1/8"

1/2"

1/8" 3/4"

1/2"

13/16"

3/16"

**MOVEMENT
PLATE**

2-7/8"

1/2"

1/8 x 1/8"
ROSEWOOD
BORDER

3-1/4"

1/8"

ACTUATING
PIN

5/16"

1/4"

1/8"

1/4"

1/2"

UPPER
SHELF

2"

1/2"

LEVER ARM

BEVEL
EDGE

GROOVE FOR ACTUATING PIN

FRONT

3/16 x 7/16 x 3-1/2"

ASSEMBLY

FALSE DRAWER FRONT   BEVEL

BACK PLATE   13/16"

may vary from those of the model used in the prototype.)

• *Finish.* To finish your jewel box fill any imperfections with a wood paste, using colors to match adjacent wood. After sanding, dust thoroughly and apply five coats of clear lacquer diluted 20 percent with lacquer thinner. Allow each coat to dry completely, then sand lightly with 8/0 paper and dust with a tack-rag. Finally rub down the last coat with pumice and water, follow with rottenstone and water and wipe away all traces of powder.

Attach the hardware, line the drawers and top tray with velveteen glued over cardboard, then attach the base and hinge the lid to the box. Finally, install the movement and pin.

MATERIALS LIST	
Amount	**Description**
5 sq. ft.	Thuya veneer
1 sq. ft.	Rosewood veneer
1 sq. ft.	Avodire veneer
1	Floral inlay (M111A)
15 ft.	¼" inlay border (56)
3 ft.	⅜" inlay border (6)
2 sq. ft.	¼" hardboard
2 sq. ft.	¼" birch plywood
3 sq. ft.	⅛" birch plywood
1 sq. ft.	¼" Honduras mahogany
1 pc.	¾ x 6 x 36" rosewood
1	Single-tune Swiss musical instrument
1 pr.	Narrow 1½" butt brass hinges
6	Brass knobs
1	Miniature brass hinge
1 pc.	.016 x ½ x 2½" brass sheet
Misc.	Red velveteen (for lining), white glue

Note: Rearrangement of parts on the movement panel may be necessary to compensate for different locations of trip wires in various movements.

Jewel boxes

■ RUMMAGING AROUND in a large dresser drawer for a tiny cuff link or earring is silly, but we all do it. How much smarter it would be to have one of these handsome large jewel boxes handy.

The miniature version of a full-size chest shown above appears to have nine individual drawers. Actually it's a fooler, it has only three. But they're long ones which make them all the more perfect for handkerchiefs, checkbooks and passport cases.

While having only two drawers, the other jewel box shown also serves as an overnight caddy for holding the contents of one's pockets. Recesses in the top provide shallow trays for parking such things as a comb, a watch and wallet, loose change and a money clip.

Only choice cabinet woods should be used for such elegant boxes and nothing but your best craftsmanship. The box shown above was made of cherry; the other, of walnut. Both were hand-rubbed to a beautiful semiluster finish. The drawers are lined with plush velveteen.

The recessed top of the walnut box shown and detailed here is a full inch thick. If you have trouble finding this thickness, you can build it up by gluing ¼-in. fir plywood to the bottom of ¾-in. walnut. The plywood will not be seen when the top is faced with the ⅜-in. strip across the front.

The stunning cherry chest is actually the simpler of the two. The dadoes for the two notched shelves are stopped ¼-in. from the front, while the bottom dado runs through. The ⅛-in. back joins the sides in rabbets. The flush-fitting drawers differ from the others in the way the sides join the fronts.

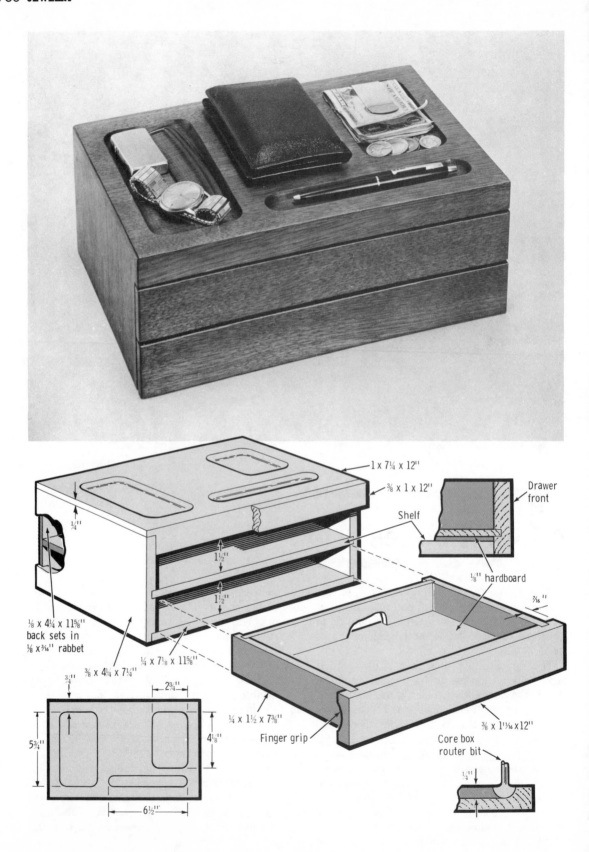

1 x 7¼ x 12''

⅜ x 1 x 12''

Drawer front

Shelf

¼''

1½''

1½''

⅛'' hardboard

⁷⁄₁₆''

⅛ x 4¼ x 11⅝''
back sets in
⅛ x ³⁄₁₆'' rabbet

¼ x 7⅛ x 11⅝''

⅜ x 4¼ x 7¼''

¾''

2¾''

5¾''

4⅛''

6½''

¼ x 1½ x 7⅜''

Finger grip

⅜ x 1¹¹⁄₁₆ x 12''

Core box
router bit

¼''

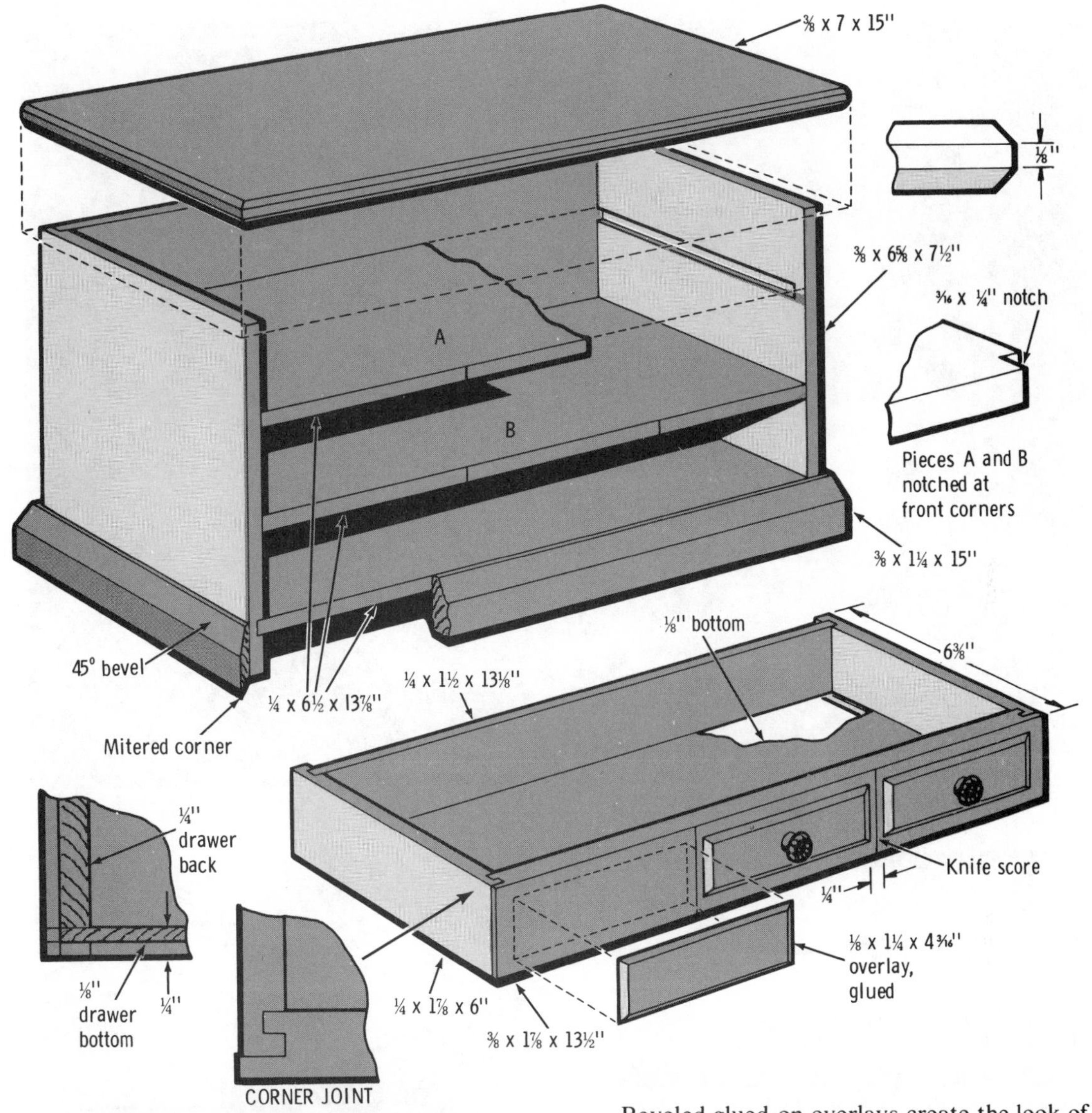
⅜ x 7 x 15''
⅛''
⅜ x 6⅝ x 7½''
3/16 x ¼'' notch
A
B
Pieces A and B notched at front corners
⅜ x 1¼ x 15''
45° bevel
¼ x 6½ x 13⅞''
¼ x 1½ x 13⅛''
⅛'' bottom
6⅝''
Mitered corner
¼'' drawer back
Knife score
¼''
⅛'' drawer bottom
¼''
¼ x 1⅞ x 6''
⅜ x 1⅞ x 13½''
⅛ x 1¼ x 4 3/16'' overlay, glued
CORNER JOINT

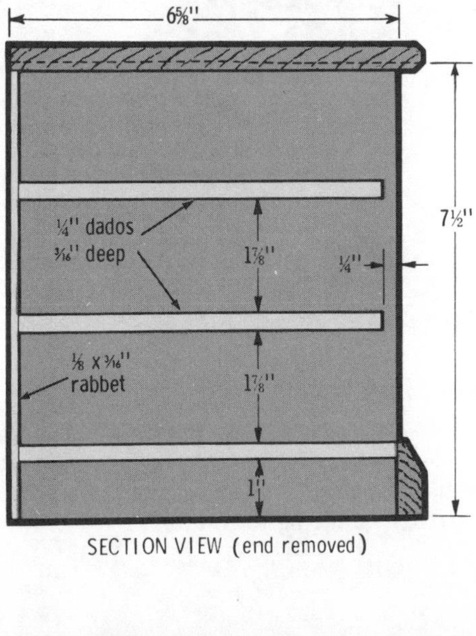
6⅝''
7½''
¼'' dados
3/16'' deep
1⅞''
¼''
⅛ x 3/16'' rabbet
1⅞''
1''

SECTION VIEW (end removed)

Beveled glued-on overlays create the look of individual drawers. Knife cuts scored across the faces of the drawers, as well as the dividing rails, make the illusion even greater. Actually, the drawers are set in ⅛ in.

The top can be pinned to the sides with short dowels or glued in ¼-in. dadoes cut on the underside. In the latter case, the height of the end members is made ¼ in. greater than that dimensioned. The back is likewise made ¼ in. higher to fit a stopped rabbet cut along the rear edge.

When you have the chest completed, sand the surfaces glass-smooth, using progressively finer grades of garnet paper. Sand the drawers before adding the overlays. Finally, stain and finish as desired, then drill the holes for tiny knobs.

Joinery— a short course

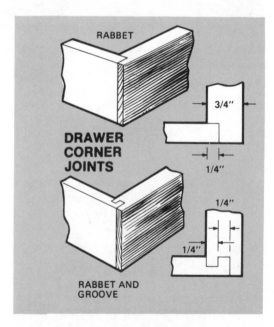

RABBET

DRAWER CORNER JOINTS

3/4"

1/4"

1/4"

1/4"

RABBET AND GROOVE

■ MAKING WELL-FITTED, properly designed locking joints is essential to woodworking. Shaping them is a matter of practice. Joints must be designed to hold a project together. The simplest joinery may involve no more than cutting and putting two pieces of wood over one another, then gluing or nailing the two pieces together. To sharpen your woodworking skills, you should work to master about a half-dozen joining techniques that have been engineered to hold your project pieces together so they won't twist, check or warp.

Butt joints

The most basic type of joinery involves butting two boards together. Sometimes a rabbet, tongue-and-groove splines or dowel pins are used to strengthen the basic butt joint.

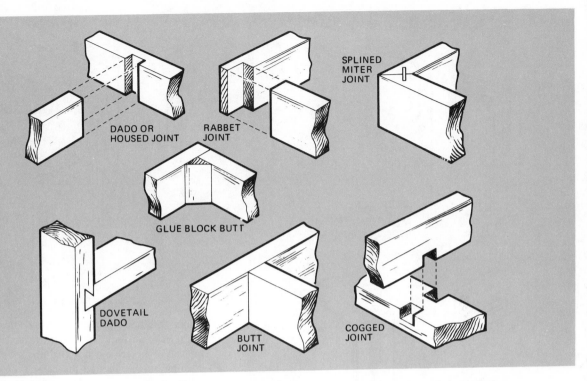

DADO OR HOUSED JOINT

RABBET JOINT

SPLINED MITER JOINT

GLUE BLOCK BUTT

DOVETAIL DADO

BUTT JOINT

COGGED JOINT

Lapped joints

In a lapped or halved joint, half of one component is mated with half of another so the original thickness of each is maintained at the joint. A variation on this joint is a mitered joint, in which each half is cut at a 45° angle to join the other.

Mortise-and-tenon joint

The mortise-and-tenon joint has been used more than any other in woodworking, and there

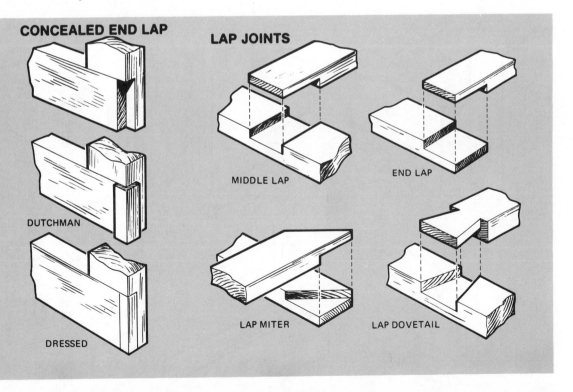

CONCEALED END LAP

LAP JOINTS

DUTCHMAN

DRESSED

MIDDLE LAP

END LAP

LAP MITER

LAP DOVETAIL

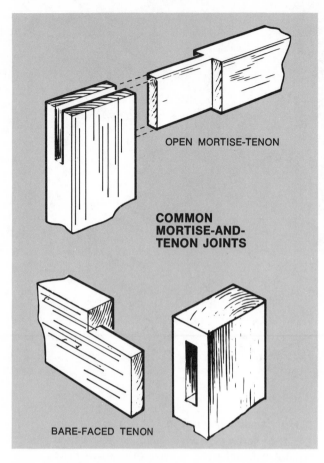

COMMON
MORTISE-AND-
TENON JOINTS

OPEN MORTISE-TENON

BARE-FACED TENON

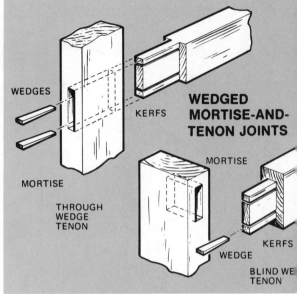

WEDGES

KERFS

WEDGED
MORTISE-AND-
TENON JOINTS

MORTISE

MORTISE

THROUGH
WEDGE
TENON

WEDGE

KERFS

BLIND WE
TENON

are many variations. Early examples of this joint can be seen in ancient Egyptian furniture.

One end of a piece of wood is shaped to fit into a matching hole in another piece.

Variations on the simple mortise-and-tenon include the pinned tenon, which uses a peg to secure the joint, and the tusk tenon, which uses a wedge.

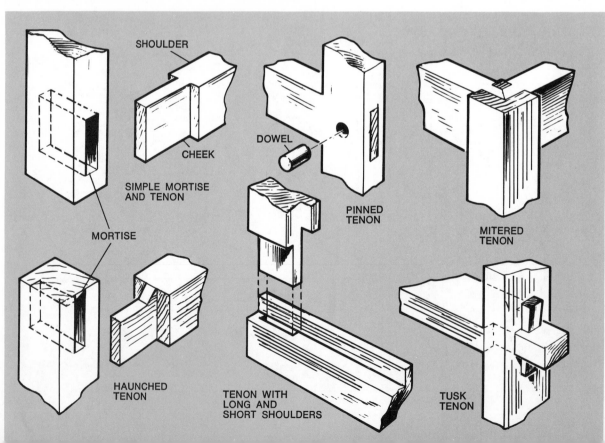

SHOULDER

CHEEK

DOWEL

PINNED
TENON

MITERED
TENON

SIMPLE MORTISE
AND TENON

MORTISE

HAUNCHED
TENON

TENON WITH
LONG AND
SHORT SHOULDERS

TUSK
TENON

Doweled joints

Doweled joints are alternatives to mortise-and-tenons. In early days, dowels were also used to reinforce joints across the grain. Most doweling is now done with prepared round rods in various lengths. The glue escapes are milled in. You can make your own by cutting a V-shaped glue relief groove.

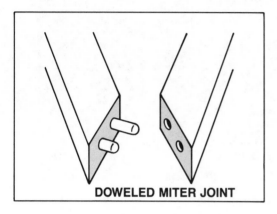

DOWELED MITER JOINT

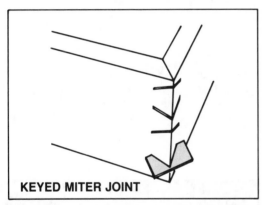

KEYED MITER JOINT

Dovetail joints

Dovetails are used to join box sides at corners and drawer fronts to sides. There are many variations of dovetail corner joints and three basic types. The first is the *through dovetail,* where tails and pins go through the other piece and both sides are exposed. In the *blind dovetail,* fingers stop short of going all the way through, so the joint is completely hidden. The third is the *lapped dovetail,* where the joint is concealed at one side.

Rabbets

A rabbet is a recess cut along the edge of a piece of wood to form an L-shape. It is used mainly in cabinet construction. The rabbet joints are commonly used on end or on edge to strengthen a corner joint. This increases glue area for better adhesion; also, if the unglued boards swell or shrink, light won't pass through.

Dado and grooves

A dado is similar to a rabbet, except it is used anywhere but at the edges of a board. A *groove* is a recessed cut, with the grain; a *dado* is a similar cut across the grain. Both provide a recess into which a second piece fits. Dado and groove joints increase contact area and provide mechanical holding power.

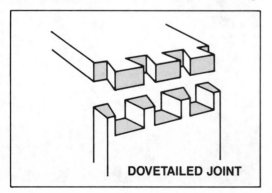

DOVETAILED JOINT

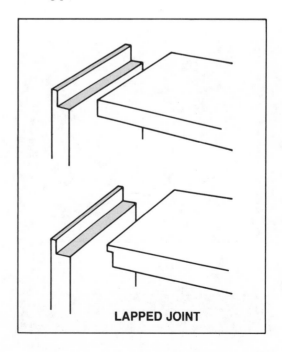

LAPPED JOINT

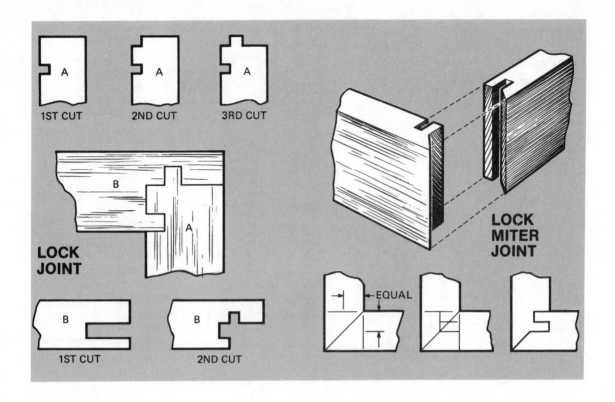

Other joints

As your woodworking skills increase, you can begin to master other joints like the lock joint or the lock miter joint, which require multiple cuts and close precision.

Tenoning jig

One of the handiest fixtures you can make for cutting tenons on a table saw is a tenoning jig.

The jig is designed to straddle and slide along the saw fence so you can safely make cheek cuts

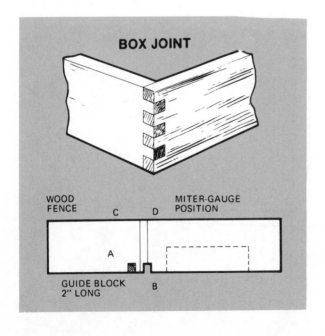

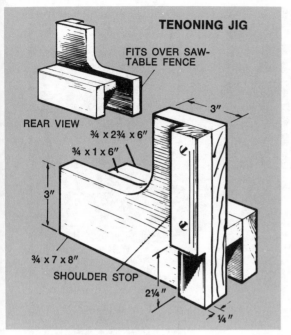

DESIGNED TO STRADDLE a saw fence, this homemade tenoning jig lets you cut accurate-fitting tenons safely on narrow stock. Jig is made from scrap and work is clamped to it.

on narrow pieces. Work to be tenoned is placed against the shouldered stop on the jig, clamped and then passed through the saw. Then the work is turned around and the cut is repeated to make the second cheek cut, and finally the work is turned end for end to cut the opposite tenon. Cheek cuts on a tenon are generally made after the shoulder cuts, and general practice in making a simple mortise-and-tenon joint is to cut the tenon first, then the mortise. While the tenon can be formed on the table saw, the mortise has to be cut with a mortising chisel on the drill press. An exception would be an open-end mortise.

Box joint jig

One of the many variations of the basic types of dovetail joints is the box joint. Similar to the dovetail joint, the box joint makes a neat-looking corner joint and is exceptionally strong since it represents lots of gluing surfaces. To make the jig, you start with a ¾-in. wood auxiliary fence, which is screw-fastened to the miter gauge. Then the regular saw blade is removed and replaced with a dado blade. In most cases the width and depth of the cut is equal to or slightly less than the thickness of the stock. Make initial cut A in the wood fence, then remove it from the miter gauge.

Mark the position of second cut B so it is spaced the same width as cut A, and at the same time mark lines C and D, centering them as shown. Nail a little square of wood 2 in. long in cut A to provide a guide pin, and finally attach the wood fence to the miter gauge and make cut B.

Mating pieces of stock are set against the fence, the edge of one piece set even with line D and the edge of the second piece even with line C (see photo). Now pass the offset work across the saw. To make the second cut, as well as the third and succeeding cuts, carefully shift the work so that the cut just made sits over the guide pin, and again pass the work across the saw. Repeat the operation along the entire width of the stock.

When making any kind of joint, it is always important to take your time and do careful work. Solid, precise cuts and edges will make your project last many years.

Do-it-yourself joinery

Mastery of joinery comes with practice. Once mastered, good joinery will produce professional-quality work. The following articles discuss several common joints and their variations in detail; mortise-and-tenon, dovetail joints, rabbets, grooves and dadoes, as well as joints to attach legs. This information, with the illustrations, will serve as a reference as you develop your skills in wood joinery.

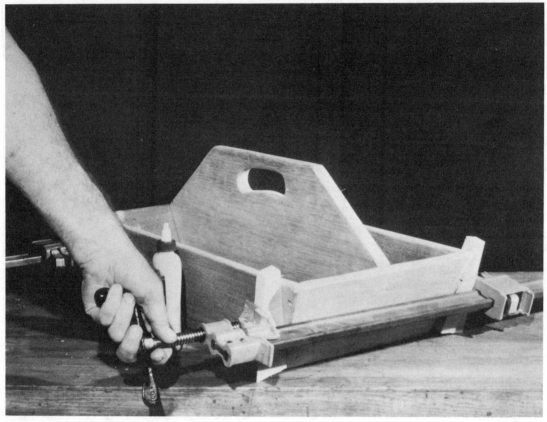

NEAT JOINTS are the unmistakable mark of a competent craftsman. Even the simple butt joint shouldn't be sold short; it's often used effectively in such projects as this antique toolbox reproduction.

Fine wood joinery you can master

■ THERE ARE A number of important steps in every woodworking project—from purchasing the stock through planning, cutting, sanding and finishing. But it's safe to say that quality of the joints is as important as any other phase of woodworking.

You may be a master of fine finishes, but a beautiful, hand-rubbed look will not conceal sloppy joinery. Ncr will it strengthen the piece. The fact is, poor joinery is the major reason for failure (deterioration) of homebuilt (and commercially manufactured) furniture.

Five important joints

Though there are countless joints to suit every conceivable joinery problem, the plain truth is that you will probably use five joints most of the time. The most commonly used joints include:

- Butt.
- Rabbets and dadoes.
- Dowel.
- Lap.

We will cover all of these joints in this article. You will learn the basics of joinery and some professional tips to use in your projects.

Mastering joinery

In simplest terms, professionals learn by practice. And practice is the quickest route to craftsmanship for you, as well. You can use scrap materials to perfect your skills with the more advanced joints—those that call for deft work with a chisel, for example. If you work at joints only when you're faced with making one for a project, mastering joinery will take you time, at best, and it may elude you completely, at worst.

In the long run you'll save time if you practice diligently on scraps.

Take advantage of the professional tricks offered on these pages. As every craftsman knows, they are mastered by experience and by working with other skilled woodworkers.

Points to remember

Here are a couple of basic points to remember:
● The butting members of a joint should be smooth. The very smoothness of mating pieces increases the resistance to pull apart. Think of the last time you tried to separate two pieces of glass. Chances are you had to *slide* one off the other—you couldn't *pull* them apart.

● Never load a joint with glue. Students are always shocked when we demonstrate just how little glue a professional uses in a joint. Apply the glue to both surfaces, then spread it thin with a clean stick, dowel, or brush. Excessive glue will *not* make the joint stronger. In fact, it can actually result in a weaker joint.

Too much glue also ensures considerable glue squeezeout, which is sure to ruin the looks of your handiwork. Even though you may not see

HOW TO MAKE BETTER BUTT JOINTS

THIS IS a typical butt joint, with one member simply abutting the other. Here, one piece is placed to project slightly to give an architectural shadow-line. The nails are driven at an angle for strength.

SCREWS GIVE an even stronger butt joint than nails—but glue is still used. To hide screwheads, counterbore holes to accept dowels. If looks don't matter, turn screws into countersunk holes.

SCREWS INTO end grain provide minimal holding power. Insert a dowel (partially installed here for clarity) to eliminate any chance of screw pulling out of joint.

THERE ARE many methods—plus commercial hardware—for strengthening a butt joint. A shopmade block such as this is installed using nails or screws through predrilled holes. Or you can use metal corner braces or irons.

YOU CAN USE a plywood gusset on a butted corner if appearance is inconsequential and its surface mounting won't interfere with function of the case. Outside edges must be perfectly square (90°), and aligned with abutted pieces to ensure a square finished project. Use glue and ringed nails.

ANOTHER version of a wooden corner block: Because this one has longer legs it gives greater stability. Shape allows easy installation.

MAKING RABBETS AND DADOES

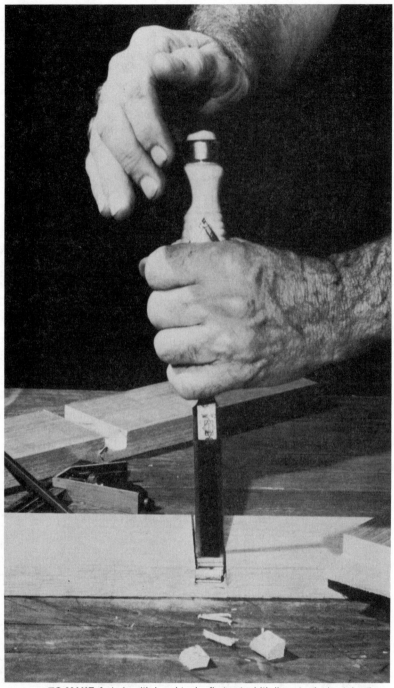

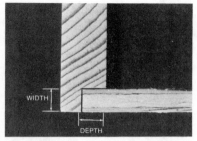

A RABBET joint is a form of butt joint, but its L-shape gives it greater strength. The edge rabbet width is equal to the thickness of the stock to be inserted into the rabbet; the depth can be anywhere from one-third to three-quarters of the stock which is being rabbeted. For this example, ½-in.-thick plywood is joined to ¾-in. stock, so rabbet was cut ½ in. wide by ⅜ in. deep.

WITH FENCE moved away from blade, saw notch is clearly shown. This stunt lets you "bury" part of the dado head in the "fence."

TO MAKE A dado with hand tools, first cut width lines to desired depth with a fine backsaw. Then use a sharp chisel to clean out interior portion.

USING A router and a rabbet-cutting bit is the fast and easy way to make a rabbet. Make certain cutter is sharp. In soft woods you should make at least two passes; make the first pass with cutter set for half depth. On hardwood, cut it in approximately three or four passes with the cutter set for one-quarter depth on first pass.

TO CUT a rabbet on table saw, always make edge cut first. This way you'll have maximum support for workpiece.

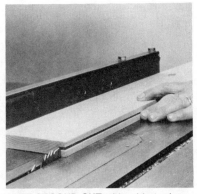

MAKE SECOND CUT with rabbet edge *away* from fence. For both cuts, blade should be elevated just to clean out corner of cut, and no more.

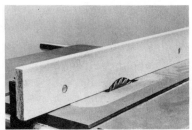

YOU CAN CUT a rabbet in one pass by mounting your dado head set on table saw. For safety, add wooden auxiliary fence, as shown here, to the rip fence. Position it with no more than half of the wood over the lowered cutters. Start the saw and slowly raise the head of the dado until you have cut a semi-circular notch.

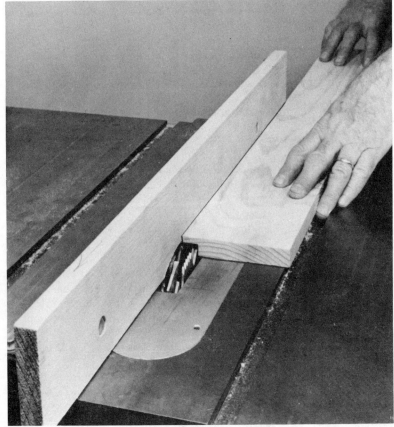

WITH THIS METHOD of making a rabbet in one pass, the work is fully supported and hands are away from the cutters. Use a pusher stick to complete the cut. For photo clarity, the blade guard is removed from saw in these pictures.

TO CUT a blind (stopped) rabbet you must add a wooden auxiliary fence with a pair of start and stop blocks clamped to it; notice the shape of start block. By rounding off the front corner, you automatically create an aid to help you lower workpiece (arrow) onto the spinning blade.

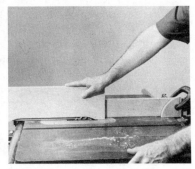

BOARD IS pushed through until it comes to rest against a stop block. At this point you should either turn off the saw and wait for blade to stop or back workpiece up a few inches and carefully lift it off. Don't attempt to lift board off table the same way it was lowered on to the spinning blade.

the glue squeezeout, it seals the wood to prevent stains and finishes from penetrating.

About butt joints

Because the butt joint is the simplest of all, many beginning woodworkers sell this type of joint short. There are times when a butt joint is quite adequate.

For example, in cabinetmaking, cases are often joined using reinforced butt joints. And butt joints are extremely common in household carpentry as long as they are executed precisely in craftsmanlike fashion.

Butt joint disadvantages

A case can be made against butt joints, of course; the biggest disadvantages are:
● Because of the minimal contact area (glue surface) between members, a butt joint is one of the weakest joints in woodworking.
● Because a butt joint leaves end grain exposed, it is not the best looking option in joinery.

It is obvious that the woodworker must consider the pros and cons of a joint on every project tackled. You would not, for instance, use a butt joint and leave end grain exposed on a fine piece of walnut furniture. On the other hand, you will often use butt joints when recreating Early American furniture, especially the primitive type created by the settlers.

Making butt joints work

● In almost every case, you should beef up a butt joint by adding a corner strengthener. You can make adequate wooden braces or you can use commercial corner braces.
● An end butt joint is the weakest of all because one of the joining pieces is end grain (as in the toolbox). One good stunt is to thin your carpenter's glue slightly with water and to precoat the end grain. The wood will suck up the thinned glue like a blotter. When it's dry, you can proceed with the joint, using the glue as it comes from the bottle.
● Though edge-joining (gluing up two or more narrow boards to create a wide one) is usually done using dowels in the edges, there are times when the dowels can be eliminated. If the wide board will be contained on all four sides in a rabbet, for example, you can frequently do an adequate job by using corrugated fasteners.

Glue and clamp

The usual technique, after spreading a scant amount of glue on the mating surfaces, is to align the boards and hold them rigid with a number of bar clamps until the glue dries. Next day, the clamps are removed and the glued-up board is placed on a solid, flat surface, hidden side up. The corrugated fasteners are driven into the board to span the joint and close it permanently.

If the board ends will be concealed in a rabbet, it's also a good idea to drive in a corrugated fastener at each end—into the end grain—spanning the joint.

A weaker joint

The important rule to remember is that corrugated fasteners should be used only where they will not be seen. Don't think that the resultant joint is as strong as a doweled joint; it isn't.

Study the pictures showing six typical butt joint applications. The rules depicted are basic for butt joints and should be added to your woodworking techniques. Remember that a nail driven at an angle, for example, holds better than one driven straight in. Also remember that, generally, you should bore lead (pilot) holes to avoid splitting, even in softwoods, because you are usually working near the end of a board.

About glue blocks

A glue block of one type or another should be used to reinforce a butt joint's glue line whenever possible. For thick stock the glue block can be shaped like those shown, but for thin stock, it is generally better to use a strip of wood for the length of the joint (because the screws used are so short). A glue block can be used outside the joint, if placing one inside will interfere with the case's operation. For example, the joint between a cabinet side and an overhanging countertop could require an outside block. If the block were placed inside, it might interfere with drawer operation.

Finally, if more than two members are being butt-joined, it is often possible to create an interlocking joint by careful placement of the pieces. If three boards join to form a corner, the corner will be stronger if each board is joined to the other two.

About rabbets and dadoes

A rabbet is an L-shaped cut made in one board to receive another. Whether the cut runs with the grain or across the grain, it is called a rabbet.

Because a rabbet increases the gluing surface

of the pieces being joined, the joint is considerably stronger than a butt joint. A typically good use for a rabbet joint is in mounting a cabinet's back panel.

Nomenclature

Dadoes and grooves are U-shaped cuts made across the face of a board. If the cut is across the grain, it is called a dado; if with the grain, it is called a groove. As with the rabbet cut, the width of the cut matches the thickness of the piece being inserted into the dado. The depth is generally one-half the thickness of the piece being plowed. In some cases, the dado is cut deeper, but be aware that this can weaken the joint.

Though a dado gives a strong joint, the general criticism is that it isn't an attractive joint. Thus, when using dadoes in a cabinet, the usual practice is to add stiles and rails to hide the plowed joints. Dadoes and grooves, like rabbets, increase the strength of the joint because of the greater gluing surface.

Cutting a rabbet

When there are just one or two rabbets to cut, it is generally done using a combination blade on the table saw, and a two-step cut.

For safety reasons, it's important that you always follow the sequence shown in the photos. Done this way, the workpiece has maximum support and there is less chance of an accident with the saw.

However, when you have a number of repetitive rabbets to cut, you can speed up the job considerably by installing your dado head set on the table saw. Make certain you add the wooden auxiliary fence, as shown, so the cut can be properly made (with the edge being cut next to the fence).

Most shops create such fences and install them on the saw fence, using flathead machine bolts and wingnuts. The hardware is kept with the fence; the fence is stored on the wall when not in use.

Using hand tools on rabbets

A rabbet can be shaped using a handsaw with the workpiece clamped in the bench vise. In general, it is best to use a stiff-bladed backsaw for accuracy of cut.

Accuracy is a must, so also use a clamped-on guide for the saw to ride against. Make the first cut, then rotate the work in the vise to make another cut to clean out the rabbet.

Some craftsmen prefer to make the first cut with a saw, then clean out the waste with a chisel.

Similarly, dadoes can be cut using hand tools. Again, the width lines are cut to the desired depth using clamped-on guides; then the waste is carefully cleaned out with a chisel (see the photo).

Stopped or blind rabbet

A stopped or blind rabbet joint is not visible at the ends. It can be done either of two ways:
● You can make your rabbet cut through the board, then fill the ends with carefully cut filler strips, after the boards are joined.
● You can make a stopped cut on your table saw, as shown in the photos. To do this, you must locate the start and stop points for the board being cut.

The easiest way to do so is to crank the blade to cutting height and hold a piece of scrap alongside the blade. You can see with fairly good accuracy just where the start block should be placed so the cut will start at the desired point, and where the stop block should be placed to stop the cut where wanted.

Position the blocks and clamp them securely to the fence. Make a test cut in scrap and adjust the blocks if necessary. When you're satisfied with locations, you can cut the actual workpieces.

The rounded portions left at the start and finish of the cut are then cleaned out (squared) with a chisel, tailoring the work to suit the board entering the rabbet.

Tips for making stopped cuts

We have probably made thousands of blind rabbet cuts, but it wasn't until the photography session for this story that we came up with the idea of rounding over the start block, as can be seen in the photo. The rounded section makes it safer and easier to lower the board being cut.

To make the blind cut, start the saw and hold the workpiece firmly against both the fence and the start block with its outboard end held well above the blade. Keeping fingers away from the blade, slowly lower the workpiece into the spinning blade until it rests flat on the tablesaw surface. When it does, slowly push the work forward until the far end contacts the stop block.

Removing the cut piece

There are two methods for removing the cut piece: 1, You can back it up slightly with blade spinning, carefully raise the far end clear of the

MAKING JOINTS WITH DOWELS

DOWELING IS THE surest way to strengthen a joint in wood. The type shown is commercially prepared with glue-escape channels machined in and chamfered at both ends. Joint here uses hidden (blind) dowels.

blade and lift it off, or 2, you can turn off the saw and wait until the blade stops before lifting it off. In either case, work carefully.

Chances are you will turn to doweling more than any other method when you want to beef up a joint's strength. Dowels can be used in almost any joint from butt to mitered—the techniques for using them remain basically the same. The important thing is to master the basics. Once you get fundamentals under your belt, the more sophisticated joinery techniques will come easily during your practice-with-scrap sessions.

Working with dowels

If you intend to seriously pursue woodworking to build your own furniture, cabinets and the like, you must master dowel joinery. In the beginning, you can work with dowel centers (in fact, these are often the handiest tools in the shop, even after you may have more advanced

equipment on hand). However, as your workshop production increases, so will your need for the quicker and more accurate doweling jig.

The usual practice with dowels is to select a diameter that is about half the workpiece thickness: It should *never* be greater. Thus, for example, you would use a ⅜-in. dowel with ¾-in. stock; a ¼-in. dowel with ½-in. wood, and so on.

Commercially made dowels

The easiest way to use dowels is to buy the commercially made versions (see photo). These are 3 in. long, chamfered both ends, and come with escape air and glue channels routed in. (The chamfered ends make it easier for you to insert the dowel.)

If you have a lot of doweling to do, you can hold down cost somewhat by buying dowel rod by the 3-ft. length and cutting lengths to suit the job. If you choose this course, remember to cut

WITH HOLES accurately marked, they can be bored in the second piece to complete the joint.

DOWEL CENTERS are an inexpensive—yet accurate—way to ensure perfectly aligned mating holes for dowels. Always locate and bore holes in end grain first (see text). Then butt work against a straightedge, as here, slide piece to be marked (arrow) against the centerpoints and press the boards together firmly.

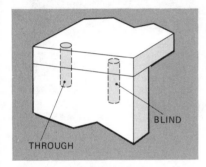

DOWELS IN butt joint make it considerably stronger. Through dowel is stronger of the two, but blind dowel is used to make joint invisible from the front.

A DOWEL JIG—the preferred method for handling a dowel joint. To start, clamp parts to be joined securely in vise. Then use a square and a pencil to mark the dowel locations on the edges of both boards.

NEXT, LOCATE hole centers, using a combination square. Here, on ¾-in. stock, square's blade projects ⅜ in. Make certain hole centers on both boards are marked from the same surfaces; that is, surfaces that line up.

BORE HOLES using appropriate bit in portable drill and a doweling jig. Position jig with its registration mark in line with first line drawn. Properly positioned bit guide will ensure that hole is bored at center of the cross marks. Make certain that the jig is rotated 180° in order to bore the mating hole.

IF YOU MUST bore a number of dowel holes along the centerline of long boards, using a portable drill and a guide makes the task much easier—and you can be sure of on-target holes. Next, dowel centers will be used to locate the dowel holes on the board to be edge-joined to the board shown in the photo.

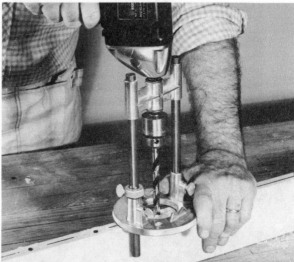

TECHNIQUE OF MAKING AN EDGE LAP JOINT

EDGE LAP actually consists of a dado cut made across a board edge, rather than its face (often called a notch). If you are making just one or two joints, start by making the shoulder cuts, then make several saw kerfs in between, as shown here. Finish the cleanout with a chisel. If you have a lot of edge laps to cut, it's faster to make the notches by mounting a dado head on the saw and making one pass.

the glue-escape channels and to chamfer the ends. We do the first by raising the table-saw blade a scant amount (maybe ½ in.) and feeding the rod in, before cutting pieces to length. Cut about half the rod, lift it off the saw, then repeat for the remaining half length. Finally, cut the pieces to length.

Chamfering can be done with a sander or plane, or very quickly in a pencil sharpener.

Aligning dowel holes

Obviously, if the dowel holes aren't aligned, the two pieces of board they are in won't be, either. For that reason, always do your marking from the same side of the board. For example, mark what will be the underside on the two boards being joined—then do the measuring for center for both boards from the *same finish surface*. This way, should your mark be off a scant amount on the first board, it will be off the same amount—in the same direction—on the second. This is especially important when working with dowel centers, or a doweling jig.

Using dowel centers

After locating dowel hole positions on the first board, bore the dowel holes. Then insert the appropriate-size dowel centers into the newly-drilled holes, and press the two boards together. Make a light match mark before separating the two boards. Remove the board and bore holes in the second edge.

The holes should be bored first in the end grain when joining an end grain to another edge, since an end grain doesn't have a uniform surface; that makes it likely the center point will hit a hard or soft spot and move the mark ever so slightly. When this happens, of course, the resulting joint won't be flush.

Tap in the dowels

Apply glue sparingly to the dowels and insert them into the holes in one of the boards. You'll probably have to tap the dowel lightly with a mallet to get it halfway home. Using a brush or small-diameter stick, apply glue to the remainder of the board edge—and remove all excess glue

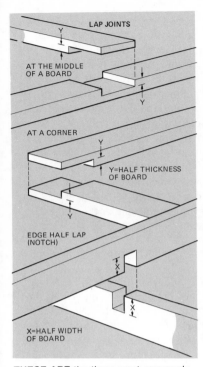

USING SQUARE and the stock itself, mark width of notch on first piece at the desired location. Repeat this step on the mating piece of wood.

NEXT, EXTEND combination square to a length equal to half of the width (of boards to be notched) and lock it in place. Then use the square to mark the depth of cut on all of the pieces to be cut. Accuracy is a must.

THESE ARE the three most commonly used lap joints. Surface lap joint lacks holding power and, if strength is important, should be reinforced with hardware. The edge lap (or interlocking) joint is solid by itself.

YOU CAN CUT notches by hand, using a fine crosscut saw or backsaw. Clamp the workpiece in a vise and use a simple, U-shaped wooden block as a guide to keep saw on a straight cutting line when you are making the two end or shoulder cuts.

USE SHARP chisel, with its bevel edge facing waste side, to remove material from notch. In soft woods, you can rap the chisel with your hand; for hardwoods, mallet taps are best. Chisel out only a small section of scrap at a time.

TO NOTCH edge lap with table saw, affix a small piece of masking tape to table in front of blade. Elevate blade to equal notch depth and make test cut in scrap. Then, holding test piece firmly against miter gauge, back latter up and turn off saw. Use a sharp pencil to mark blade position.

WHEN THE NOTCH is almost fully cleaned out, test-fit the pieces to avoid overcutting and sloppy fit. Use chisel or file to clean out additional material.

MAKE THE two outside cuts first, using tape registration marks as your guide.

WELL-EXECUTED edge laps produces a joint that is nearly invisible, with no gaps between boards and edges that are flush.

MAKE REPEATED passes over spinning blade to remove waste.

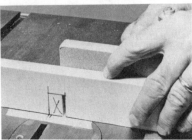

from around the dowels. Align the two boards and join them by applying pressure with clamps. Bar clamps are best when edge-joining boards and scrap wood should always be placed beneath a metal clamp's jaws to prevent damage to the workpiece.

Often, edge-joined boards have a tendency to "curl" or bow. You can prevent this with clamps and additional boards *across* the bow. Apply clamp pressure until you can spot slight glue squeezeout along the glue line (joint) and set the work aside to dry for 24 hours.

Using a doweling jig

With one of these, you can become an expert with dowels in less time than you might imagine. There are several types of doweling jigs available.

To use the jig, you first lay out the hole locations with a square, as shown. Use a pencil with a very fine point, or a scratch awl. Then place the jig on the workpiece after aligning its registration mark with the mark you just made on the wood. When it is aligned, lock the jig in place with its clamping device.

Next, the appropriate-size bit guide is lined up and locked in place. (In the example shown, the ⅜-in. guide is in place on the jig because we wanted to bore ⅜-in. holes.)

Measure the distance from workpiece edge to top of jig and add 1⁹⁄₁₆ in. to determine the drill bit's total depth of penetration. Put your depth stop on the bit at that point—a masking-tape flag works fine—and stop drilling when the flag touches the top of the jig.

Since the jig is, in effect, a round tunnel that your bit must follow, you will get the most accurate holes using spur or brad point bits. These aren't as fast drilling in wood as spade bits are, but the results will be more accurate because the bit is in close proximity to the guide.

Several professional tips

● Always use at least two dowels in a joint to gain maximum strength. A pair also prevents the joint from pivoting.
● Make certain you use only hardwood dowels. The commercial type available at lumberyards and home centers will be either birch, maple or hickory.
● Keep your dowels in a dry, well-ventilated place. If you work with a wet dowel it will shrink as it ages and, consequently, will cause an unwanted loose joint.

About lap joints

Webster's New World Dictionary describes a lap joint as "a joint made by lapping one piece or part over another and fastening them together." And that, in simplest terms, is exactly what a lap joint is. There are many variations, however.

The most common lap joint is the surface lap, such as those found in a garden trellis. A surface lap joint is not strong; the contact (glue) area won't resist twist or lateral stress. For this reason, it's the usual woodworking practice to create half-lap joints, as shown in the drawing. Here, the wood parts are notched to half-thickness so the joint will be an interlocking one, and the surfaces will be flush.

Full lap joint

Occasionally, you'll need to use a full lap, generally when one of the parts is thinner than the other. The seat cut (dado) is made in the thicker piece to accommodate the thinner piece. Thus, for example, if you want to join a ½ by 3½-in. member to a length of 5/4-in. stock, you would cut a 3½-in.-wide dado to a depth of ½ in. in the 5/4-in. lumber. As with a half lap joint, a full lap should also produce members that are flush when they are joined.

An end lap occurs in framemaking (i.e., doors) and the rabbet cuts are determined using the mathematics shown in the drawing.

Cutting an end lap joint

When cutting a frame lap joint (rabbet), always make the shoulder cut first, then the cheek cut. The workpiece should be clamped in a vise and, to ensure accuracy, you can clamp a depth stop block to the saw. In general, you should leave the line when making a joint—you can always take some more off with a sharp chisel. Too much removed, however, means that the resulting joint won't be flush.

Rotate the workpiece in the vise to make the second (cheek) cut. Repeat the steps for the second member. Test the parts for fit and, if necessary, clean out additional stock from mating cheeks for a flush joint.

To cut end laps on a table saw, you can use a combination blade and two cuts. Again, make the shoulder cut first, using your miter gauge. Then turn the stock on edge and use the rip fence to make the cheek cut. Work carefully when making a cheek cut and keep the part being cut out away from the fence (to ensure the stock riding the table throughout.)

Use a tenoning jig

It is better and safer to use a tenoning jig to make the cheek cut when using a conventional blade. With one of these, the work is securely clamped and there is no chance of kickback. In fact, if you own a tenoning jig, you can make an end-lap rabbet cut in one setup by using a dado head and elevating the cutters to desired lap width.

If the stock being joined in your end lap joint is wider than 2½ in., use a dado head, rather than a conventional blade, to make the cut.

To do it, install the dado head set on the saw and set its cutters to project the desired distance. Using your miter gauge, make the shoulder cut first, then carefully make repeat overlapping passes over the cutters to clear out the remainder of the joint.

More professional tips

● When creating a notch or dado with a table saw—whether using blade or dado head set—it's not uncommon to have saw ridges remain on the cheek. Since these must be cleaned out later with a chisel to ensure a tight joint, cut a hair less than required.

● Professionals always keep stock of the same size and dimension on hand for test cutting and fitting. Use this stock for testing all saw settings, and so on before cutting your expensive, project material.

Half laps

There are many variations of half lap joints, the simplest of which is shown in the drawing—the half lap at the middle of a board.

Here, in both members, the dados are cut to equal the stock's width and half its thickness. The cutting can be by hand or with power, as shown in the photo.

Edge half laps

These are the same as a conventional half lap except that the cutting is done in the board edges, rather than on the surface. As a result, the dados are much narrower and deeper. Frequently called notches because of this shape, the joint produced is a strong interlocking one. This is a conventional assembly technique in certain projects—that is, egg-crate or wine-rack, construction.

Again, the shoulder cuts are made first, then the area between is cleaned out. The shoulders can be cut using a handsaw and a miterbox, or the work can be clamped in a vise. The cutout should be carefully marked, using a square as shown, but, if you don't trust your ability to stop sawing at a marked line, clamp a depth stop to the saw.

After making the shoulder cuts, make one or two additional kerfs in the field (see photo), then clean out the notch with a sharp chisel. To do it, position the work on a flat, solid surface and hold the chisel with its bevel toward the waste area. Give the handle a sharp rap with the palm of your hand to clear the waste. Finish clearing the notch, using the chisel with a paring action.

Edge half laps on a table saw

Edge laps are particularly easy to cut on the table saw if it's equipped with a dado head set. If you are cutting the notches for a project requiring many members—such as a wine rack—you can save time by ganging the marked members together and cutting them all at once. Remember to clamp the pieces securely so they can't shift during the cutting step.

About joints in general

● Always use a quality glue in your joints. Apply the glue sparingly, and *never* spread it on too thickly.

● Before gluing, make certain you test-fit the parts. Put the pieces together and clamp them "dry" to locate problems. A lap joint should have tight shoulders and the members must be flush. If you must join a great number of parts that have been notched, you can avoid confusion during final assembly by making light pencil match marks during your dry assembly.

● Whenever possible, use hardware (screws or nails) for additional joint strength. Though the lap joint is a considerably stronger joint than the plain butted joint, it too can use some help in the form of screws or nails.

● If you do produce a less than perfect joint, all is not lost. If you plan to paint the project, you can fill small voids, using a paste consisting of fine sawdust mixed with white glue. Or, use a quality wood filler.

For projects to be stained, you won't get off so easily. If the sloppy joint is just a hairline loose, you *may* be able to conceal it using a wax putty stick (of the type intended for wood paneling) after the piece has been stained and varnished, or some other finish has been applied.

But, as a woodworker, you should always remember that the quality of the joints in your projects is a true measure of your skill as a woodworker.

Dovetail joints

■ A DOVETAIL with its flared sections is one of the most attractive woodworking joints. Its interlocking parts along with resulting increased gluing surfaces also give this joint great strength.

Laying out the joint accurately is all important and takes careful attention—both with hand and power tools.

Laying out the dovetail

It's best to draw the dovetails on the board, cut them out, then use the piece as a pattern for tracing the outline of the pins on the mating member.

(Note: Although most dovetail joints end with partial pins at the outsides, joints ending with partial tails don't seem to show any weakness due to the variation.)

Use a sharp, hard lead pencil, or preferably a knife to mark the cutting lines. Make sure both boards are square.

Estimate the number of spaces needed on the first board to accommodate the pins in the sec-

ond. To do this, first decide the width of the pins; a full pin should equal about a three-quarter thickness of the board. Multiply the pin width by 2½ to find the distance from center to center of the pins. Divide the board width by this distance and you will get the number of pins needed. However, since there are usually half pins (plus ⅛-in. width) at the outside, subtract 1 from the answer you get to allow for them.

Begin by marking off the extra ⅛-in. width of the partial pins on the board that will contain the tails. Depth of the cut-out spaces should equal the thickness of the mating board, so mark off that depth on edges and faces of the dovetail board. Actually, it's best to add ¹⁄₃₂ in. overall to allow for a final flush sanding to size.

To mark off the already determined center-to-center distance of the pins between the ⅛-in. borders, lay a ruler diagonally across the space until the dimension is easily divisible by the number of pins you want. Then with a square at the joint (edge of the board) draw parallel lines to mark the centers of the pins. Continue the lines on the end of the board.

On the edge of the board mark off a ⁵⁄₁₆-in. width for each pin centered on the centering

---

Computing dovetail joints

CERTAIN PROPORTIONS are best to assure sturdy dovetail joints: 1. Plan the widest point on the pin face to be about three-quarters of the wood thickness. 2. Make the distance from center-to-center of the pins about 2½ times the pin width. 3. The two end pins are usually half the width plus ⅛ in. for strength. 4. Pins and tails can be of equal width, but some craftsmen prefer pins about one-third the width of the wide end of the tail and not less than ¼ in.

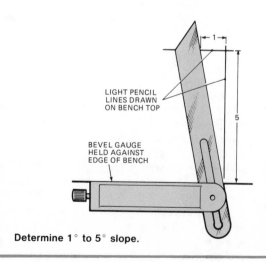

LIGHT PENCIL
LINES DRAWN
ON BENCH TOP

BEVEL GAUGE
HELD AGAINST
EDGE OF BENCH

Determine 1° to 5° slope.

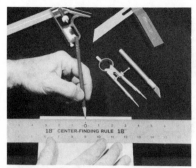

MAKE LAYOUT with ruler, square, bevel square, knife and dividers.

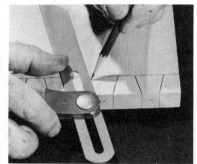

HOLD PENCIL at angle so point rides firmly against straightedge.

USE FINE-TOOTH dovetail saw to cut joints. Cut on waste side of lines.

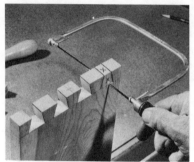

USE COPING saw to make the bottom cut that clears out the waste wood.

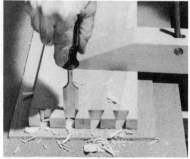

SHARP CHISEL dresses cuts to lines. Clamp and work against a scrap board.

TRACE TAILS with knife to outline pins. With a square carry lines to board face.

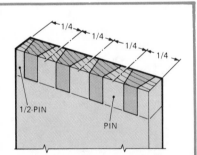

Board divided to make four tails.

THE FINISHED joint should fit snugly. Note partial tails here.

NOTCHED BLOCK bears clamp pressure *only against dovetails* when gluing.

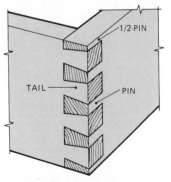

For strength, board with pins is drawer front, tails on sides.

FOR HALF-BLIND doves, cut tails, then saw pins at upward angle.

CLEAR WASTE with chisel and mallet on crossgrain, just chisel on endgrain.

Half-blind dovetails made with router

CUT HALF-BLIND doves with a router, template, base guide and dovetail bit.

CLAMP SIDE and end member into the template with pieces butting each other.

Single dovetail made with table saw

USE TENONING jig to make many cuts. Make first cut, then reverse piece.

TURN WORK perpendicular. Use miter gauge and clamped block to cut waste.

WITH HIGH stop block, set gauge at right, then left angles for pin cuts.

Half-lap dovetail made with radial saw

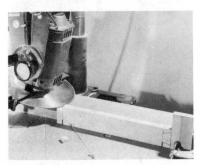

MAKE TWO straight cuts into each end. Set blade at angle to cut off waste.

REDUCE the face of the dovetail by making repeated passes of the saw.

ESTABLISH cutting lines by tracing them against tail overlap with knife.

lines. Then set a bevel square to a 1° to 5° angle (as shown in the drawing). Draw the sides of the pin spaces (which are the tapered sides of the tails). Cut out the space for the pins as follows, leaving the tails.

Dovetails cut by hand

Secure the piece in a vise and use a fine-tooth back or dovetail saw to cut the tapers. Cut on the waste side of the line, leaving the line exposed.

Cut out the spaces between the pins and finish off with the chisels. This phase will be more tedious because you'll have to work the chisel into the angled bottom corners.

Test for fit frequently. A good joint will require light tapping. Next use a coping saw to cut across the grain to remove the waste.

Use a razor-sharp chisel—the largest one that fits the opening—to trim the tails. Then clamp this section to the mating piece and use a *knife* to outline the pins.

FEED router against template fingers to cut joint parts together.

RESULT: a perfect dovetail that could hardly be duplicated by hand.

ASSEMBLED half-blind routed dovetail. It's excellent for drawers, cabinets.

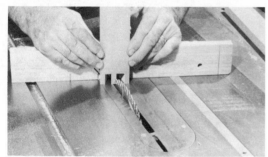

REMOVE THE WASTE between pins by repeated passes over the saw. Keep thumbs out of the blade path!

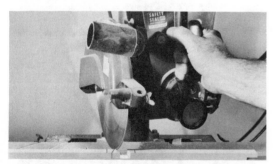

SET THE SAW arm at the required angle. Then raise the arm and make passes with an elevated blade.

Apply glue to all surfaces. Use a notched block that will bear pressure only over dovetail portions of the joint. Attach clamps. Sand surfaces flush after the glue has dried.

Half-blind dovetails hand-cut

A half-blind or lap dovetail doesn't show on the front surface. It is used for drawer fronts or cabinet corners. The procedure for making a half-blind dovetail is similar to that for making a through dovetail. However, the tails are shallower—equal to the amount of the lap dimension of the mating piece; and the pins aren't cut through to the front surface.

Cut dovetails, then place the board on the mating member, set back the required amount from the face. Scribe cutting lines. Pins are not cut through—saw them at an angle for a partial cut. Don't cut beyond the guide lines.

To remove waste between the pins, clamp work to the bench and hold a chisel perfectly perpendicular. Cut a V-notch at the back guide line. Then alternately chisel with and across the grain to remove the waste. Use a mallet when cutting across the grain.

Dovetails on table, radial saws

A single through dovetail is used to join narrow-width framing members. A tenoning jig makes cutting the tails on a table saw easier, or you can use a miter gauge. Half-lap dovetails are used to join cross members.

Dovetailing with a router

A router is ideal for making dovetail joints. A guide (collar), dovetail bit and a relatively simple attachment that clamps the mating pieces together in a template reduces the task to its simplest form.

Set up the accessory attachment and insert the guide. Install bit and adjust cutting depth. Clamp butted pieces into the attachment. Run router from right to left to break the front edge of the stock so it won't split at edges. Then, working from left to right, guide it around the template.

Dowel joints

FOR MAXIMUM shear strength, dowel diameter should be half the thickness of the wood being joined and dowel length six to eight times its diameter.

■ THE FAMILIAR dowel joint, now centuries old, is a good substitute for a mortise-and-tenon or a tongue-and-groove joint and, of course, is superior to screws and nail joinery. And the investment in power tools for doweling is less than that for mortising tools.

A dowel butt joint isn't quite as strong as a mortise-and-tenon, but that difference can be minimized by using good doweling techniques and modern plastic-resin glue. That's why you find that most of today's commercially manufactured furniture is doweled. With equipment that is presently available and a little know-how your projects can be just as strong.

Alternate annular rings

Before starting any doweling operation there are a few points to have in mind. When you're edge-gluing stock, the annular growth rings in each board (they're visible on the ends) should curve alternately. Viewed from an end, for example, if rings on the first board arch, they should dip on second board—and so on. Such care to alternate the rings will offset the tendency of each board to cup and give you a flat overall project. Also, when the edges of two boards touch, the middle two-thirds of the joint should show a sliver of light. Then, when the bar clamps draw the joint tight, the glue-line at the ends will be especially fine.

And, before picking up the drill to bore those dowel holes, sight along the edges of the boards to be joined. If a board shows even a slight bow or warp, it should be trued-up on the table saw. Doing this now will save a lot of aggravation later.

THREE WAYS to lay out dowel centers: (at top) gauge and try square, (in middle) tape and pinheads, and (at the bottom) drilled holes and dowel centers.

COUNTERSINK DRILLED holes to remove any burr that might hold joint apart, also to facilitate the board assembly and to permit excess glue to escape.

FOR MAXIMUM torque strength, use at least two dowels. For a tight joint when edge-joining boards, dowels should be more than 20 in. apart (maximum).

DOWEL CENTERS are slipped in holes bored in first board; to transfer centers to second board, both boards are lined up and tapped with a mallet.

FAST WAY to bore precise holes is with a spur bit chucked in a portable drill or drill press. Wrap piece of tape around shank as a depth stop.

STUBBY SPUR BIT won't drift from center point as metal bits often do, and it will also drill deeper than a spade bit without piercing the other side.

FOR SHOP-MADE dowel pins, measure the bored holes with a depth gauge and then mark the length. To make a neat cut use a fine-tooth hacksaw.

DOWEL SHARPENER is used to taper both ends of the dowels, simplifying the job of inserting them into the holes.

WHEN USING SOLID dowels, cut a groove the length of each pin to let the air and glue escape. Without such relief the wood may split.

TO SCORE a spiral along dowel, you just apply a sliding-rolling pressure on the dowel with the edge of a small mill file. Spiral helps spread glue evenly.

As a final step before drilling, lay out the boards to be joined to get the most pleasing grain design. The ultimate, of course, (for perfectionists) is to achieve a finished surface that appears to be one wide plank. Here you will be restricted by how careful you were when you selected the planks at the lumberyard. In other words, don't let the yard man foist material upon you exactly as he takes it from the pile. Take a good look at the grain of each piece before you make your purchase.

Choosing correct size dowel

The six basic doweling steps are shown in the photos. As a rule of thumb for the size dowel to use, the dowel's diameter should equal one-half the thickness of the wood being joined. As for dowel length, you are safe if you cut it about six times the dowel diameter. Thus, to join ¾-in. stock, you would use ⅜-in. dowels cut to 2½-in. lengths.

Lay out the holes to be bored so that they are registered perfectly. You can do this with one of the simple hand methods or, if your shop projects call for a lot of doweling, with a dowel jig. Five models are shown and countless other versions are probably available.

Assembling board

With dowel pins cut to length, chamfered and kerfed for glue ooze-out, assembly can be started. Dribble glue in the holes in the first board and tap the dowels in place. After applying glue to the board-edge and mating drill holes, press the boards together and finish with bar clamps. Don't overtighten clamps or you might cause bowing. Finally, wipe off all excess glue before it sets and set the workpiece aside overnight to dry. Next day, use a plane if necessary to smooth the surface and then finish the job with a thorough sanding.

If you take a reasonable amount of care along the way, you will have professional-looking—and fitting—dowel joints at a minimum cost.

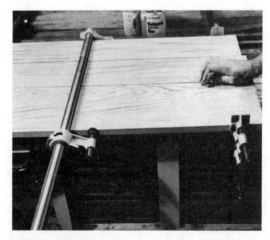

BOARDS ARE edge-joined by dripping glue in each hole, twisting the dowels in place and applying glue to the mating edge. Then clamp boards until glue sets.

FIVE JIGS THAT MAKE DOWELING EASIER

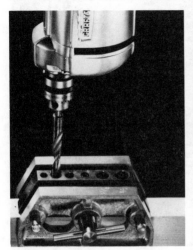

SELF-CENTERING drill guide that boasts a heat-treatment feature will accommodate six drill sizes ranging from ¼ through ½ in.

DRILLING IS SIMPLIFIED with this jig because its revolving turret adjusts quickly and eliminates loss of loose sleeves or parts.

THIS DRILLING JIG provides the means to drill properly aligned holes to depths of 1¹/₁₆ in., adapts to various board thicknesses.

INEXPENSIVE VERSION available at building-supply houses and hardware stores, this unit accommodates most common dowel sizes, requires registration lines made with a try square.

WITH A GUIDE CLAMPED in position, the top bar of this dowel jig swings two ways for perfectly matched holes. The C-clamp is not included in the set.

Rabbet and dado joints

DADO AND RABBET joints increase contact area and thus are stronger than butt joints. For dado joint, one board should be a slip fit in the groove—too tight a joint can produce undue stress.

■ AFTER THE BUTT JOINT, it's a pretty safe bet that the two most common joints in woodworking are the rabbet and dado.

The L-shaped rabbet is used in most simple projects, cases, boxes and the like. If you work with sharp cutters and saw blades, you can produce very neat-looking rabbet joints using either two passes on the table saw, or a rabbet cutter in your router. Plough the groove slightly wider than needed and sand smooth the $\frac{1}{32}$ in. or so overhang after the glue has dried.

The U-shaped dado provides gripping action of the groove and more gluing surface than the butt joint.

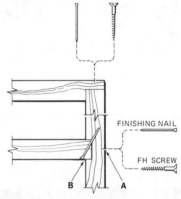

FINISHING NAIL

FH SCREW

B   A

JOINTS ARE SECURED with glue and either nails or screws (dowels can be substituted if preferred). Dado can be fastened using method A or B. The latter technique makes the joint fastening invisible.

A BUTT JOINT is weak because fasteners have a tendency to pull out. Dowel in the second piece, at 90° to fastener, eliminates this problem (left). Joint to the right was cut away on the bandsaw to show how screws get a bulldog bite.

NEATER-LOOKING drawer joint is obtained by ploughing an L-shaped rabbet across ends of drawer front and sides. Joint is stronger because end-grain contact for both pieces is cut by 50 percent.

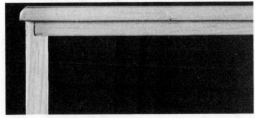

SIMPLE WAY to attach a drawer front: Sides are let into L-shaped rabbet in front and nails are driven through sides into and parallel to front to assure maximum resistance against pullout.

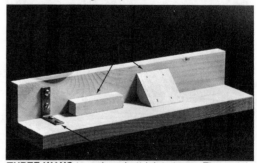

THREE WAYS to make a butt joint strong. The metal corner brace is store-bought. The triangular and square glue blocks can be made right in the shop. Use these where they won't show.

Attaching legs

■ YOUR CHOICE of methods for attaching legs depends on the piece of furniture and its style. If you're building a simple modern chest or slab table, you can usually get by with purchased legs that screw into their own mounting plates. But if you're reproducing or refurbishing a period piece, you'll most likely have to go to hand joinery.

The dozen methods sketched on these pages cover most means of attaching legs to rails and aprons or flat undersides. Say you want to build a workbench that won't jiggle or "walk" when you plane stock or do some hammering. For this, use the butt joint with a drawbolt to join the legs to the rails of the frame. You'll get a job that will take the roughest usage—even without bracing or gluing.

In making a cabinet or table with turned legs, use rails-to-legs joints with mitered, wedged or draw-pinned tenons.

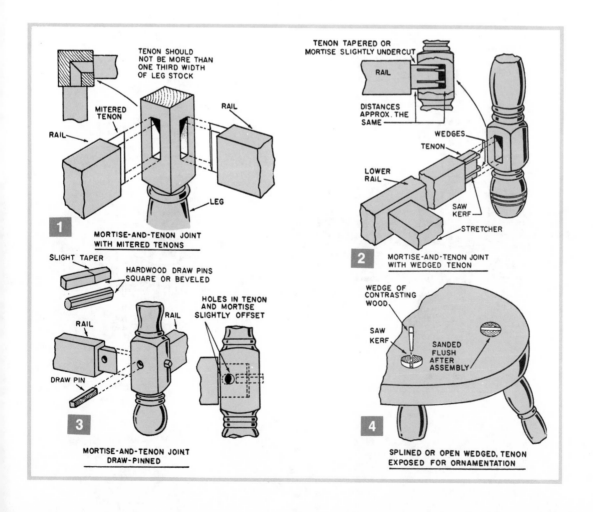

1 — MORTISE-AND-TENON JOINT WITH MITERED TENONS

TENON SHOULD NOT BE MORE THAN ONE THIRD WIDTH OF LEG STOCK

MITERED TENON

RAIL

LEG

2 — MORTISE-AND-TENON JOINT WITH WEDGED TENON

TENON TAPERED OR MORTISE SLIGHTLY UNDERCUT

RAIL

DISTANCES APPROX. THE SAME

WEDGES

TENON

LOWER RAIL

SAW KERF

STRETCHER

3 — MORTISE-AND-TENON JOINT DRAW-PINNED

SLIGHT TAPER

HARDWOOD DRAW PINS SQUARE OR BEVELED

HOLES IN TENON AND MORTISE SLIGHTLY OFFSET

RAIL

DRAW PIN

4 — SPLINED OR OPEN WEDGED, TENON EXPOSED FOR ORNAMENTATION

WEDGE OF CONTRASTING WOOD

SAW KERF

SANDED FLUSH AFTER ASSEMBLY

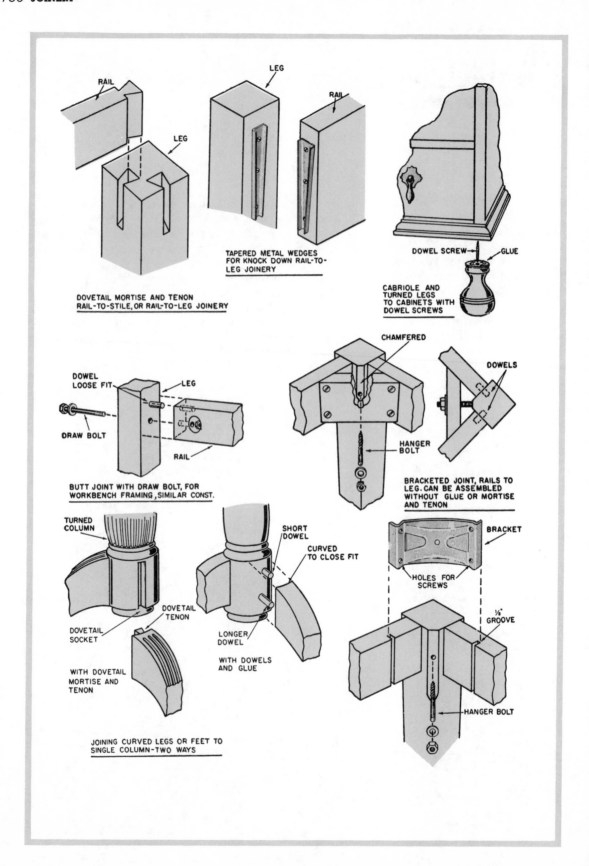

RAIL

LEG

LEG

LEG

RAIL

TAPERED METAL WEDGES
FOR KNOCK DOWN RAIL-TO-
LEG JOINERY

DOWEL SCREW

GLUE

DOVETAIL MORTISE AND TENON
RAIL-TO-STILE, OR RAIL-TO-LEG JOINERY

CABRIOLE AND
TURNED LEGS
TO CABINETS WITH
DOWEL SCREWS

DOWEL
LOOSE FIT

LEG

DRAW BOLT

RAIL

CHAMFERED

DOWELS

HANGER
BOLT

BUTT JOINT WITH DRAW BOLT, FOR
WORKBENCH FRAMING, SIMILAR CONST.

BRACKETED JOINT, RAILS TO
LEG. CAN BE ASSEMBLED
WITHOUT GLUE OR MORTISE
AND TENON

TURNED
COLUMN

SHORT
DOWEL

CURVED
TO CLOSE FIT

BRACKET

DOVETAIL
TENON

HOLES FOR
SCREWS

DOVETAIL
SOCKET

LONGER
DOWEL

⅛"
GROOVE

WITH DOVETAIL
MORTISE AND
TENON

WITH DOWELS
AND GLUE

HANGER BOLT

JOINING CURVED LEGS OR FEET TO
SINGLE COLUMN-TWO WAYS

Jointer use guide

■ A JOINTER MAY not be the *first* tool to buy for a woodworking shop, but it is a versatile woodworking machine and a valuable complement to a table or radial-arm saw.

A jointer is used primarily to smooth rough, irregular board edges prior to edge-gluing into panels or ripping on a saw. Cut the boards with the straight, joined edge against the saw fence. You can also use the jointer like a planer to smooth the faces of narrow boards.

Jointer mechanics

A jointer is simple in both design and operation. A base supports two independently adjustable tables. Positioned between the tables is a cylindrical-steel cutterhead that holds removable knives. The cutterhead is driven by a belt connected to the motor. An adjustable, tilting fence guides the workpiece and a retractable guard covers the cutterhead. *Caution:* In several photos the safety guard has been removed for photo clarity. Never operate any power tool unless the protective guards are in place.

The jointer's front, or infeed, table is adjusted for the depth of cut. The rear, or outfeed, table is, for most operations, positioned at the same height as the knives to support the workpiece as it passes the cutterhead.

A jointer requires few adjustments, but these must be made carefully to obtain optimum performance.

First, check the position of the knives in the cutterhead. The knives must align with each other and be level with the table. To check knife alignment, clamp two 12-in. steel rules to a wood block that's about 1 in. narrower than the cutterhead. Unplug the power cord and remove the guard. Next, elevate the rear (outfeed) table slightly above the knives. Then, clamp the rules/block assembly to the rear table, so the rules overhang the knife edge by ⅛ in.

Now lower the jointer's outfeed table until the rules touch the knife. If only one of the rules makes contact, then the knife isn't level with the table. Loosen the locking screw and adjust the knife so it touches both of the rules. Ro-

tate the cutterhead and align the remaining knives to the same ⅛-in. marks.

Next, check the front (infeed) table's depth-of-cut scale and indicator, or pointer, for accuracy. Set the jointer for a ⅛-in.-deep cut. Then, accurately scribe a ⅛-in. line on a test board. Make a partial cut and see if the line and cut match. If not, adjust the table as required. Repeat until the cut is exactly ⅛ in. Now set the indicator to ⅛ in.

Check the accuracy of the tilting fence using a square. At 0° the fence should be exactly perpendicular (90°) to the front table. Also, check the fence at 45°. Adjust the fence and indicator as necessary.

CHECK KNIFE ALIGNMENT by clamping two steel rules to the rear table, as shown. Pencil wedged alongside cutterhead keeps it from rotating. Adjust knife to touch both rules.

USE A SQUARE to check the accuracy of the tilting fence. Fence should be exactly perpendicular (90°) to the table. Adjust the automatic stops and indicator, if necessary.

MAKE A TEST CUT in a pre-marked board to check the accuracy of the depth-of-cut scale. If cut and line don't match, adjust the front table accordingly, and set indicator.

KEEP KNIFE EDGES KEEN between sharpenings by honing them with a fine stone. Clamp pulley so that stone rests on knife bevel. Paper around stone protects table.

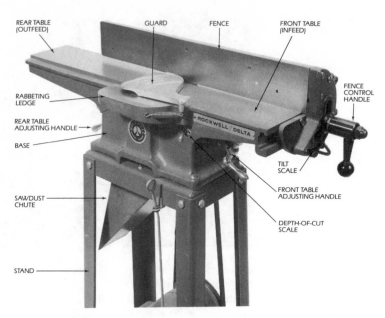

REAR TABLE (OUTFEED)
GUARD
FENCE
FRONT TABLE (INFEED)
RABBETING LEDGE
REAR TABLE ADJUSTING HANDLE
BASE
FENCE CONTROL HANDLE
TILT SCALE
FRONT TABLE ADJUSTING HANDLE
DEPTH-OF-CUT SCALE
SAWDUST CHUTE
STAND
ROCKWELL / DELTA

Jointer operations

Edge-jointing is the most common of all jointer functions. First, determine the wood grain direction. Whenever possible, you should cut with the grain, not against it.

Next, hold the stock firmly on the front table and against the fence. Advance the workpiece into the cutter and onto the rear table while applying pressure with your left hand. As the rear end of the stock nears the cutter, apply pressure with your right hand.

JOINT END GRAIN with slow, shallow passes. To prevent splintering the rear edge, first make a short cut, then turn the workpiece around and make a full pass, as shown.

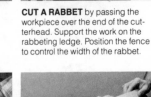

CUT A RABBET by passing the workpiece over the end of the cutterhead. Support the work on the rabbeting ledge. Position the fence to control the width of the rabbet.

THE SAFEST WAY to cut bevels is with the fence tilted in to form a closed angle. This makes it easier to keep the workpiece in close contact with the fence and table.

HERE'S A QUICK AND EASY WAY to make an octagon: Set the fence to 45°. Then, chamfer the corners of a square workpiece. Make the same number of passes for each corner.

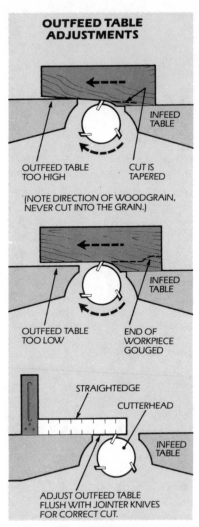

OUTFEED TABLE ADJUSTMENTS

OUTFEED TABLE TOO HIGH
CUT IS TAPERED
INFEED TABLE

(NOTE DIRECTION OF WOODGRAIN, NEVER CUT INTO THE GRAIN.)

OUTFEED TABLE TOO LOW
END OF WORKPIECE GOUGED
INFEED TABLE

STRAIGHTEDGE
CUTTERHEAD
INFEED TABLE

ADJUST OUTFEED TABLE FLUSH WITH JOINTER KNIVES FOR CORRECT CUT.

THE ILLUSTRATIONS ABOVE show how a misaligned rear, or outfeed, table affects the workpiece. Adjust the jointer so that the table is at the same height as the knives. Use a straightedge to check table height.

When edge-jointing extra long pieces, employ the aid of a helper or build the extension table shown. First, set the jointer to the desired depth of cut. Then run a long 1×4 *halfway* through the jointer to form the auxiliary fence. Screw short 1×3 sections to the bottom ends of the auxiliary fence to act as extensions of the jointer tables. Now screw through the jointer fence and into the auxiliary fence.

End-grain jointing is a little trickier than edge-jointing. Feed the work slowly and take shallower cuts to avoid kickback. To prevent the workpiece back edge from splintering when the knives exit, first make a short cut into one end. Then, turn the workpiece around and make a full pass.

Rabbeting on the jointer is possible if your

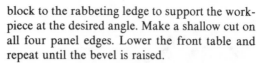

CUT RAISED PANELS for cabinet doors on the jointer with the aid of a push stick. Clamp a wood block to the rabbeting ledge to support the workpiece at the desired angle.

CUT THE CROSS-GRAIN BEVELS first; any splintering will be removed by the edge-grain bevel cuts. Then, make light, edge-finishing cuts to complete the door panel.

block to the rabbeting ledge to support the workpiece at the desired angle. Make a shallow cut on all four panel edges. Lower the front table and repeat until the bevel is raised.

Recesses are stopped cuts (cuts contained within the workpiece) that are made on board edges with the fence perpendicular to the table. First, lower both the front and rear table equal amounts below the cutterhead. Then, clamp start and stop blocks to the fence to control the recess. Next, butt one end of the workpiece against the start block and hold the front end above the cutterhead. Once the piece is set, turn on the jointer, lower the workpiece and make a short cut. Then, lift the board, turn it around and feed it in the opposite direction. This two-cut technique prevents splintering the trailing end.

Tapering stock on a jointer is a safe, accurate technique. The most common is the straight taper, which tapers the entire length of a work-

LOWER THE FRONT AND REAR TABLES equally when cutting recesses or stopped chamfers. Check the table alignment by placing a straightedge across the table tops.

TO CONTROL the length of a recess cut, clamp start and stop blocks to fence. Then, butt the workpiece end against the start block and lower it slowly onto the cutterhead.

ADVANCE THE WORKPIECE slowly past the cutterhead to the stop block. Install an auxiliary fence with extension tables, as shown, to support oversized workpieces.

HERE'S HOW to cut end tapers: Butt the workpiece against a stop block clamped to the fence. Then, slip a wood block under the raised leg end to maintain this angle.

NOW, WITH THE BLOCK NAILED to the workpiece underside, stand in front of jointer and pull the work across cutterhead. Block thickness determines the degree of taper.

AFTER TAPERING THE ENDS, cut recesses to form a furniture leg. Cut a short recess, then turn the leg around and feed it in the other direction to prevent splintering.

CONTOURING WORKPIECES into irregular, freeform shapes is possible on the jointer. First, make a series of shallow chamfer cuts to form the basic shape of the piece.

CONTINUE TO MAKE SHALLOW CUTS while rotating the workpiece slowly. Keep a firm grip on the workpiece at all times. Decrease the depth-of-cut as the piece takes shape.

FINALLY, finish-shape the workpiece with the jointer adjusted for very shallow cuts. Use the fence to guide the piece straight. Hand-sanding completes the project.

THE FEATHERBOARD hold-down is a necessity when jointing thin stock. Cut the feathers on a band saw. Clamp the hold-down directly over the cutterhead and rear table.

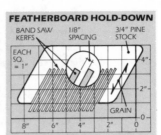

FEATHERBOARD HOLD-DOWN

BAND SAW KERFS
1/8" SPACING
3/4" PINE STOCK
EACH SQ. = 1"
GRAIN
4"
2"
0
8"   6"   4"   2"   0

piece. When tapering a board that is shorter than the front table, carefully place the front end on the rear table just beyond the cutterhead. Then slowly lower the board onto the front table and advance it past the cutterhead.

When tapering long workpieces, there are two options: add an extension table to the jointer or use the following procedure. First, divide the board into equal parts. Make each part slightly shorter than the front table. For example, if the front table is 13 in. long, divide a 24-in.-long board in two. Then, divide the desired taper into the same number of parts. In this example, to obtain a ¼-in. taper, set the depth of cut to ⅛ in. and make two passes.

Make the first pass with the division line positioned over the cutterhead. Lower the board and advance it past the cutterhead. Next, place the workpiece front end on the rear table just beyond the cutterhead. Lower the board and make a full-length pass. The resulting taper will equal ¼ in.

MAKE A WIDE PUSH BLOCK for cutting tenons. Assemble the block using glue only. Masking tape applied to fence indicates where to stop advancing the push block.

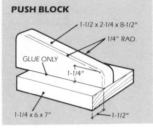

PUSH BLOCK

1-1/2 x 2-1/4 x 8-1/2"
1/4" RAD.
GLUE ONLY
1-1/4"
1-1/4 x 6 x 7"
1-1/2"

A PUSH BLOCK should always be used to surface plane boards on a jointer. Shape this block on a band saw from a 2 x 4. Add stop block to the underside with glue only.

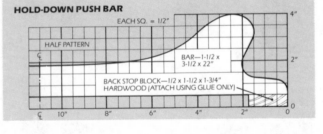

HOLD-DOWN PUSH BAR

EACH SQ. = 1/2"
HALF PATTERN
BAR—1-1/2 x 3-1/2 x 22"
BACK STOP BLOCK—1/2 x 1-1/2 x 1-3/4" HARDWOOD (ATTACH USING GLUE ONLY)
4"
2"
0
10"   8"   6"   4"   2"   0

MAKE THE THREE-HANDLE BLOCK for surface planing long stock. As the work advances across the clutterhead, shift your hand from the lead handle to the middle position.

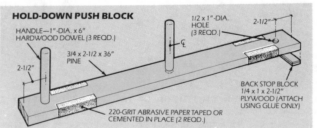

HOLD-DOWN PUSH BLOCK

HANDLE—1"-DIA. x 6" HARDWOOD DOWEL (3 REQD.)
3/4 x 2-1/2 x 36" PINE
2-1/2"
1/2 x 1"-DIA. HOLE (3 REQD.)
2-1/2"
BACK STOP BLOCK 1/4 x 1 x 2-1/2" PLYWOOD (ATTACH USING GLUE ONLY)
220-GRIT ABRASIVE PAPER TAPED OR CEMENTED IN PLACE (2 REQD.)

BUILD THIS AUXILIARY FENCE with extension tables at a 45° angle for chamfering long pieces. Note that a small cut is made in the fence center to clear the cutterhead.

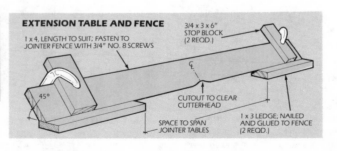

EXTENSION TABLE AND FENCE

1 x 4, LENGTH TO SUIT; FASTEN TO JOINTER FENCE WITH 3/4" NO. 8 SCREWS
3/4 x 3 x 6" STOP BLOCK (2 REQD.)
45°
CUTOUT TO CLEAR CUTTERHEAD
SPACE TO SPAN JOINTER TABLES
1 x 3 LEDGE; NAILED AND GLUED TO FENCE (2 REQD.)

The jointer also is the best tool for cutting end tapers. First, mark the workpiece where the taper is to begin. Rest the workpiece end on the front table with the starting line of the taper directly above the knives. Then, clamp a stop block to the fence against the end of the workpiece.

Now, while holding the workpiece at this angle, position a support wood block under it. Attach the support block to the workpiece with brads. Turn on the jointer, butt the workpiece end against the stop block and pull it over the cutterhead. Reposition the support block and repeat the procedure for the remaining sides.

Tenoning on a jointer is accomplished with the aid of a push block. Assemble the simple block using glue only, as illustrated. Adjust the jointer fence to determine the tenon length. Advance the workpiece past the cutterhead with the push block firmly against the fence. To prevent splintering the workpiece rear edge, first establish the tenon shoulders by sawing a kerf on a radial-arm or table saw.

Round tenons are made easily with the aid of an L-shaped block. Clamp the block, as shown, to the rabbeting ledge so that the workpiece will engage the knives on the downward rotation.

Tapering-in-the-round is a quick way to produce round, tapered furniture legs. Build the sliding jig, as illustrated, to accommodate the workpiece.

With the fence tilted 45°, shape the workpiece into an octagon. Then, mount the workpiece in the jig. Note that the locations of the pins that hold the stock determine the degree of taper. Position the rear pin lower to form the narrower, tapered leg end. Place the workpiece front end on the rear table just beyond the cutterhead. Then, lower the workpiece and make a full-length pass on the jointer. Rotate the work slightly and repeat the procedure. After a full revolution, increase the depth of cut to reduce the taper more.

CUTTING ROUND TENONS is handled easily with the aid of an L-shaped jig. Clamp the jig to rabbeting ledge. Push the work into the spinning knives and rotate clockwise.

ROUND TENON JIG

1-1/2 x 4-1/4 x 12" PINE

2"

3"

3/4 x 3 x 5" PINE

ASSEMBLE USING NAILS AND GLUE

USE THE TAPERING-IN-THE-ROUND JIG in conjunction with an auxiliary fence and extension tables (above). Mount the workpiece in the jig and slide it across the cutterhead. Rotate the stock and repeat.

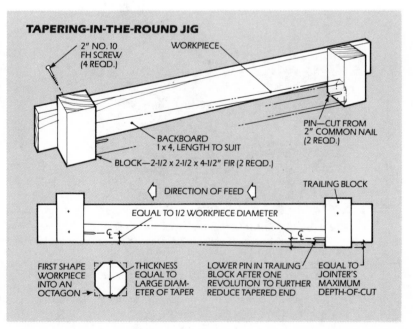

TAPERING-IN-THE-ROUND JIG

2" NO. 10 FH SCREW (4 REQD.)

WORKPIECE

PIN—CUT FROM 2" COMMON NAIL (2 REQD.)

BACKBOARD 1 x 4, LENGTH TO SUIT

BLOCK—2-1/2 x 2-1/2 x 4-1/2" FIR (2 REQD.)

DIRECTION OF FEED

TRAILING BLOCK

EQUAL TO 1/2 WORKPIECE DIAMETER

FIRST SHAPE WORKPIECE INTO AN OCTAGON

THICKNESS EQUAL TO LARGE DIAMETER OF TAPER

LOWER PIN IN TRAILING BLOCK AFTER ONE REVOLUTION TO FURTHER REDUCE TAPERED END

EQUAL TO JOINTER'S MAXIMUM DEPTH-OF-CUT

Bonus tricks for your jointer

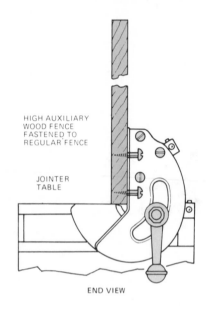

HIGH AUXILIARY
WOOD FENCE
FASTENED TO
REGULAR FENCE

JOINTER
TABLE

END VIEW

1 High fence for tall work

THE STANDARD 4-in. jointer fence should be fitted with an oversize auxiliary one to provide adequate, positive support when planing large work, as shown above. Select a perfectly flat piece of plywood, sand the face and apply a coat or two of sealer followed with a coat of paste wax to make it extra smooth. Use roundhead screws through the existing holes in the jointer fence to attach the plywood. Side pressure is essential to keep the work in full contact with the fence.

2 Shouldered tenons

SHOULDERED TENONS on narrow stock are easily handled with the aid of a backing block. This is simply a square block of 2 x 4 or the like, which is used to push the work squarely across the cutter head as you keep the end of the work firmly against the fence. If the shoulder cut is fairly deep, make the cut in two or more passes. Flop the work with each cut before lowering the front table to make the next.

3 Push block for safety

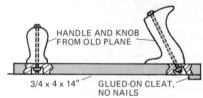

HANDLE AND KNOB
FROM OLD PLANE

3/4 x 4 x 14"   GLUED-ON CLEAT,
NO NAILS

SURFACE PLANING should never be done without using a combination push block/hold-down to keep your hands clear of the cutter head. The push block shown makes use of parts from an old hand plane, but you could also use 1-in. dowels for handles. In use, the pusher is grasped by one hand on the knob, the other on the handle. A small cleat across the end on the underside hooks over the edge of the work-piece.

4 Stopped bevel chamfer

THIS HANDSOME cut is widely used for table and chair legs, posts and general cabinetry. It is made in the same way as a common stopped chamfer with the exception that the jointer fence is tilted 45° to form a beveled cut. Use an auxiliary wood fence with stop blocks attached, and lower both tables an equal amount. Elevate the lead end of the work while resting the opposite end against the right-hand starting block. Start the machine, lower the work into the cutter, then advance it slowly until it reaches the forward stop block. Important: Use *two* hands for this operation. (One hand is shown in the photo for the sake of clarity.) The operation requires the removal of the blade guard so watch your fingers when making cut.

5 How to plane end grain

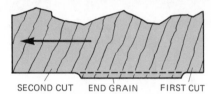

SECOND CUT   END GRAIN   FIRST CUT

PLANING END GRAIN with a jointer will usually chip and splinter the wood at the end of the cut. But not if you first make a short cut with the jointer and then reverse the work to complete the cut. The knives of the cutter head merely pass over the initial cut without cutting, resulting in a chip-free corner. End grain of a board should always be planed first, then the side grain for best results.

6 How to make novelty molding

DECORATIVE MOLDING can be produced with the jointer by making a series of cove cuts in the surface of the work. To do this, clamp a wooden stop block to an auxiliary wood fence and mark the fence with equally spaced index lines. Butt the end of the work squarely against the stop, then slowly and carefully lower it face down into the rotating cutter head. Shift and reclamp the stop for each cut. Both the front and rear tables must be lowered an equal amount for this operation. You can use your imagination to create different designs by varying the spacing of the index marks.

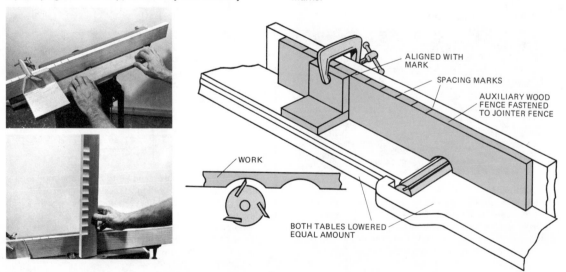

ALIGNED WITH MARK

SPACING MARKS

AUXILIARY WOOD FENCE FASTENED TO JOINTER FENCE

WORK

BOTH TABLES LOWERED EQUAL AMOUNT

7 Cutting raised panels

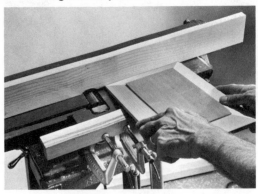

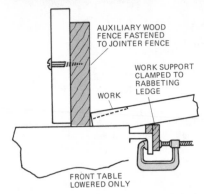

AUXILIARY WOOD
FENCE FASTENED
TO JOINTER FENCE

WORK SUPPORT
CLAMPED TO
RABBETING
LEDGE

WORK

FRONT TABLE
LOWERED ONLY

RAISED DOOR panels can be formed neatly with the jointer. First clamp an auxiliary wood fence to the jointer fence, letting it just clear the tables. Set the fence for the desired width of cut, then clamp a strip of wood to the rabbeting ledge of the rear table. This supports the wood at an angle to produce the desired amount of bevel as the work is passed over the cutter. Take small bites, about 1/16 in. at a time, and make cross-grain passes first, then the straight grain, to avoid chipping as you pass over the corners.

9 Freehand rounding

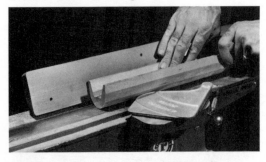

ROUND SHAPES can be formed with a jointer by making repeated passes and changing the angle of incidence with each cut. The fence is adjusted to a single arbitrary angle to serve only as a guide to keep the work moving in a straight line. The procedure is basically a freehand operation so "eyeball" your progress carefully as you work.

8 Big and little rabbets

WHEN THE JOB calls for a rabbet that must be made by planing, it's a simple operation for a jointer whether it be an edge rabbet or a surface one. You simply position the fence to set the rabbet's length or width and adjust the front table to set its depth. Rabbet depth is limited, of course, to the rabbet ledge on your particular machine, and when the depth required is greater, you will be forced to cut such rabbets on your table saw. An extra smooth rabbet can be cut with a hollow-ground planer blade. Certain dado cutters will produce a smooth rabbet too. In the case of a dado cutter, it's often necessary to add a wood facing to the saw's fence.

10 Shouldered tenons

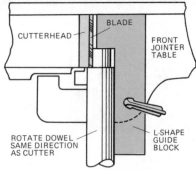

CUTTERHEAD — BLADE

FRONT
JOINTER
TABLE

ROTATE DOWEL
SAME DIRECTION
AS CUTTER

L-SHAPE
GUIDE
BLOCK

A NOTCHED BLOCK clamped to the rabbeting ledge of a jointer permits cutting round tenons on round stock. The position of the clamped block sets the length of the tenon, while the front table adjustment determines the depth of cut. To turn a tenon, push the work into the spinning cutter from the side and then slowly rotate the work in the same direction of rotation as the cutterhead.

11 How to cut stopped chamfers

A STOPPED CHAMFER can add an interesting shape to a square chair leg. Here's how it's made on a jointer. Lower front and rear tables equally. Then clamp start and stop blocks to an auxiliary wood fence to limit length of cut. Place the end of the leg against the front-table stop block and start the machine. Lower the raised end of the work into the rotating cutter and advance the work until it touches the rear-table stop block. Be sure the front-table stop block is clamped securely in place because there is a forceful kickback thrust to the work at the start of the cut.

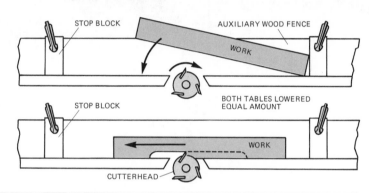

12 How to make bevels

BEVELS ARE CUT running work against a tilted fence in an "in" or "out" position. The outward tilt shown is safer because fingers are in full view. When working with wild grain, an inward tilt is needed for a smooth cut. Several passes with adequate downward and sideward pressure are usually required.

WEAR SAFETY GOGGLES

13 Tapering square stock

TO SHORT-TAPER the four faces of square stock, you pull the work over the cutterhead. Lower the front table to suit the amount of taper. Then mark stock where the taper is to start and center mark directly over the cutter. Press down so the corner of the work contacts the front table and slip a block under the raised end of rear table to hold work at an angle. Mark block location on each face with a try square, then lightly brad block to one face. To start cut, rest front end against a clamped block that prevents kickback and assures the same starting point for each pass. Rebrad block to the work for each of the four cuts.

STAND'S LEGS are splayed in two directions for vibration-free operation. Beneath the jointer is a sawdust drawer and push block shelf.

Mobile stand for a 6-inch jointer

■ THIS STURDY, vibration-free jointer stand is suitable for all 4- and 6-in. jointers. It's easy to keep clean and can be rolled into position on casters. The sawdust drawer collects chips and has handles at both ends for dumping. Casters can be quickly raised or lowered by foot levers.

Build the stand's frame first. The prototype was made of oak, but fir can be substituted if rail lumber dimensions are increased to 1½ x 2½ in. and legs to 1½ x 3½ in. Note the legs are splayed. Thus, dadoes (U-shaped notches for lower rails) and end rabbets (L-shaped cutouts for top rails) in legs must be made with 7° angle crosscuts. To lay out joints accurately, first cut the legs to

length. (Compound 7° cuts are required at both top and bottom of legs.) Next, cut rails to overall dimensions given. Then lay legs on flat surface, in proper relationship to each other.

Position the upper and lower rails and trace for the cutouts. Do the same for each face on the stand. The top edge of the upper rails (B and C) must be beveled 7° to achieve a level mount for the tool.

Mounting the jointer

All joints should be glued as well as bolted. Use 5/16-in.-dia. lagscrews where bolts are not feasible. The plywood drawer is assembled with glue and nails. For most jointers, the motor may be swung from a rod located between the top stretchers. The weight of the motor maintains the proper belt tension.

Bolting the jointer to the stand will also vary from model to model. Steel-plate and bar supports for heavy models distribute weight on rails; ¾-in. plywood will distribute weight of lighter units. Cut a hole in the plywood to allow cutter chips to shoot into sawdust drawer. In mounting a Shopsmith jointer, mounting tubes should be cut off so that they won't extend into the drawer area.

LARGE SAWDUST drawer slides easily on the angle-iron tracks for removal and emptying.

SHOPSMITH 4-in. jointer can also be accommodated by this stand that includes retractable casters.

MATERIALS LIST—JOINTER STAND

Key	No.	Size and description (use)
A	4	1¾ x 2½ x 26″ oak (leg)*
B	2	1½ x 1¾ x 38¼″ oak (upper side rail)*
C	2	1¼ x 1¾ x 12″ oak (upper end rail)*
D	2	¾ x 1¾ x 44″ oak (lower side rail)*
E	2	1¼ x 2 x 18″ oak (lower end rail)*
F	3	1 x 1¾ x 15″ oak (brace)*
G1	1	¾ x 11¾ x 15″ plywood (drawer front)*
G2	1	¾ x 11¾ x 13¾″ plywood (drawer back)*
H	2	⅜ x 15 x 24¼″ plywood (drawer sides)*
I	1	⅜ x 11⅜ x 23⅛″ plywood (drawer bottom)
J	1	¾ x 1 x 10¼″ oak (pull and stop)*
K	1	¾ x 1 x 7″ oak (handle)*
L	4	³⁄₁₆ x 1½ x 1½ x 6″ angle
M	2	¾ x 3¼ x 15½″ oak
N	4	¾ x 4¾ x 15½″ oak

Key	No.	Size and description (use)
O	4	¾ x 2½ x 4″ oak
P	4	retractable casters
Q	1	½″-dia. x 11¾″ steel rod
R	1	motor mount
S	2	⅜″-dia. x 2½″ carriage bolts
T	8	No. 8 x 1½″ fh machine screws, washers, lock washers, nuts
U1	4	⁵⁄₁₆″-dia. x 3″ carriage bolts, washers, nuts
U2	16	⁵⁄₁₆″-dia. x 2¼″ carriage bolts, washers, nuts
V	4	⁵⁄₁₆″ x 2½″ carriage bolts with Teenuts
W	12	No. 8 x 2″ fh wood screws
X	2	⅛ x ¾ x ¾ x 24½″ angle irons

Misc.: White glue, 4d nails, sandpaper.
* These are overall dimensions, pieces must be cut to fit.

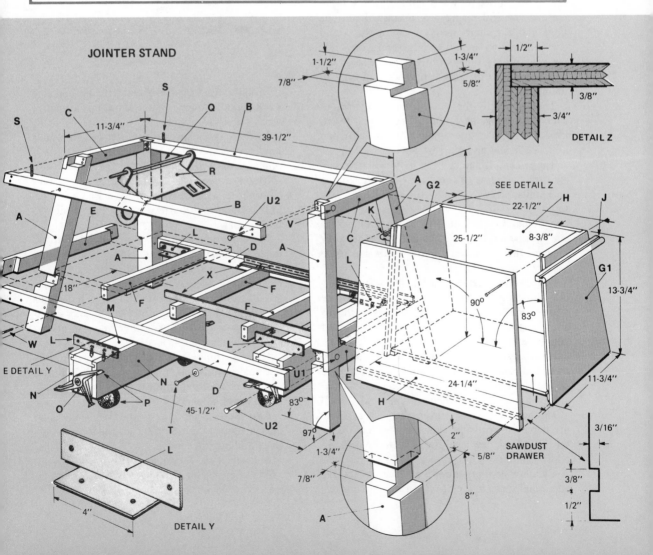

JOINTER STAND

Kitchen projects and improvements

■ A DRAB KITCHEN can be transformed with just a little work and a lot of inspiration, as these photos show.

New cabinets in this kitchen were constructed from the original pine floorboards from the attic of this Pennsylvania farmhouse. The handsome stone walls of the house were exposed and painted. A kitchen island now provides additional work space and a more open feeling. The old built-in cupboard was given light and wallpaper for cheerful display. A refinished antique table and old chairs now provide a warm and cozy new eating area. The large-scale, off-white textured ceramic tile floor brightens the room but will not show dirt, and is durable and easy to maintain.

The kitchen is the most productive area in every home. On the following pages are design ideas and remodel tips to help make your kitchen a more efficient and pleasant place.

The kitchen island you can build will give you an attractive piece of furniture for more storage and a nice place to work—with a butcher block top.

A Colonial cutlery cupboard is a clever weekend workshop project that will provide your kitchen with a handsome Early American place to store knives and forks.

Built-ins for kitchen and laundry feature rollout carts to give your household work life new wheels for efficiency and less toil. Here are ideas and construction concepts for the kitchen and laundry areas.

Hideaways for kitchen and laundry hide the clutter in cabinets that not only let you store household work but let you achieve new efficiency in both your kitchen and laundry.

The hood for an over-oven range is a sheetmetal project trimmed with wood to give your kitchen a fresh new look and drive those cooking odors outdoors.

A kitchen-door organizer is an easy way to gain additional space in a place that everyone has but is usually wasted. Designed to hang on the kitchen door, you may want to put this attractive unit in other places.

Kitchen space saver is a clever bin that adds kitchen storage space in a useful place that is often overlooked.

Mobile kitchen island rolls where you want it—right to your daily work zone. Plans for this unit include multipurpose storage—including a built-in bar.

More storage space in your kitchen can be made from places you least expect. Several projects will show you how to transform clutter and dead space into new, efficient organization.

This pantry on wheels shows how to build rolling bins that let you see and get to any stored item in your food pantry, while you can almost double the shelf space available.

Hangups for your kitchen are quick projects that make any kitchen easier to use. You'll find plans and construction ideas from knife racks to paper towel holders.

Easy projects add spice to your kitchen with an old-time grocery-bin canister set and a handsome knife and napkin caddy.

A handy rack for food-processor parts is an easy project to build and gives you a place to store those awkward parts.

The tray for your best silver is a Colonial-inspired tray and a fine workshop project resulting in an elegant table.

The turned-handle cutting board is a hardwood project that will last for years with an initial in-vestment of very little shop time.

A home telephone organizer can be built from the plans for this mahogany cabinet to store tele-phone equipment and provide a small desk space in your kitchen.

Kitchen island you can build

■ IF YOU HAVE THE NEED—but not the wall space—for additional countertop work area in your kitchen, why not consider the advantages of this attractive island work center? Besides its generous work top (more than 13 sq. ft.), this elegant cabinet will permit you to store almost all your kitchen utensils out of sight. And, from a practical standpoint, you'll have the advantage of being able to work from all four sides of a food preparation table—a luxury chefs have enjoyed for years.

The cabinet has a laminated chopping top that offers:

● A surface where foods can be chopped, pounded, cut and scraped—with cleanup afterward a snap.
● A top that can be quickly and easily dressed to almost-like-new with a belt sander in the event tool marks, cuts or scratches start to make it unsightly.
● Embossed sides of textured hardboard that

THE EMBOSSED-LEAF PATTERN gives this island work center its elegant look. Hardboard panels are available in two colors: ivory-white (shown below) and a dark-stained, walnut look.

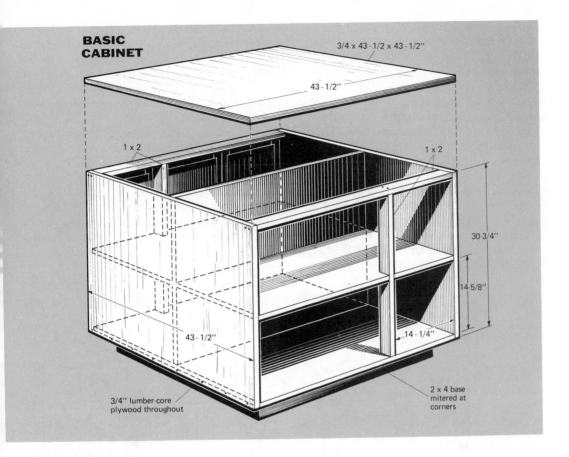

BASIC CABINET

3/4 x 43 - 1/2 x 43 - 1/2"

43 - 1/2"

1 x 2

1 x 2

30-3/4"

14-5/8"

14 - 1/4"

43 - 1/2"

3/4" lumber-core plywood throughout

2 x 4 base mitered at corners

are easy to clean and make this handy kitchen center fit into any modern decor.

Building the center. Since the cabinet rests on a base nailed to the finished floor, a mock-up—left in place for a while—is a good idea. Simply lay the 2 x 4s in the chosen location and leave them there. Then, after a couple of days of walking about the planned center, you'll know whether you have picked the best site. If you find that a mobile island would be more desirable, you can fit the base with lockable casters instead of nailing it down, but be sure to adjust the vertical dimensions accordingly.

The cabinet. Constructed of ¾-in. plywood and 1 x 3 pine, the cabinet is kept simple by using butt joints rather than grooving and letting in the members. (For example, shelves rest on one-by cleats.) For maximum strength, use plenty of wood screws and waterproof glue.

Chopping-block top. Birch or maple should be

TEXTURED HARDBOARD comes in 16 x 96-in. panels and requires no finishing. You'll find it available at many lumberyards.

your choice for the laminated top. Both hardwoods have handsome grain characteristics, are long-lasting and are extremely resistant to scratches and mars. To insure lineup for the holes in the 47 pieces that receive the threaded rods, take time to set up a jig. A simple way is to cut a 47-in. length of inexpensive material, mark off and bore the three required holes. Then use this pattern as a drilling guide. Since the holes may vary slightly from edges or ends, mark each piece as it's drilled with an arrow for up and an X at one end to keep holes matched.

With all boards cut and drilled, slip the rods through. Next, apply waterproof glue liberally to all meeting surfaces and draw the boards tight with bar clamps. (If you have good, warp-free

stock, the joints should be mere hairlines with glue oozing out evenly.) Wipe off all excess glue with a damp cloth, and set the top aside to dry overnight. Next day, counterbore the holes, cut rods to exact length, slip on the washers and run the nuts tight. Do not remove the clamps until all six nuts are fully tightened.

The embossed-leaf pattern inserts in the 12 panels are let into rabbets on the inside back edges of the stiles and rails. These can be cut and rabbeted assembly-line fashion at one time. Assemble the frames and cut the hardboard to fit. Again make match-marks in case of variations. With inserts removed, paint or stain the frames and then reassemble them. The top, of course, should not be painted.

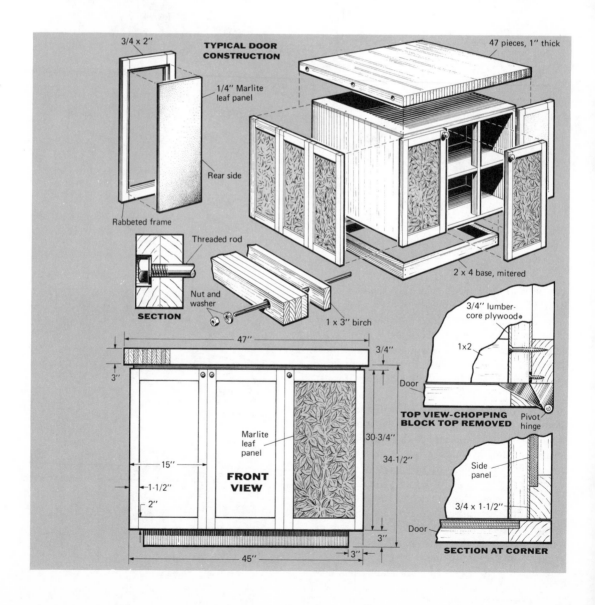

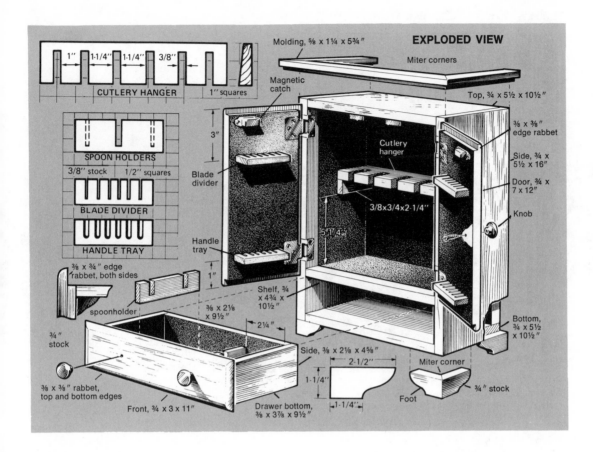

EXPLODED VIEW

Molding, ⅝ x 1¼ x 5¾″
Miter corners
Top, ¾ x 5½ x 10½″
⅜ x ⅜″ edge rabbet
Magnetic catch
Side, ¾ x 5½ x 16″
Door, ¾ x 7 x 12″
Knob
Cutlery hanger
3/8x3/4x2-1/4″
Bottom, ¾ x 5½ x 10½″
Blade divider
Handle tray
Miter corner
¾″ stock
Foot
Shelf, ¾ x 4¾ x 10½″
Side, ⅜ x 2⅛ x 4⅝″
spoonholder
⅜ x 2⅛ x 9½″
¾″ stock
⅜ x ⅜″ rabbet, top and bottom edges
Front, ¾ x 3 x 11″
Drawer bottom, ⅜ x 3⅞ x 9½″

CUTLERY HANGER
1″ 1-1/4″ 1-1/4″ 3/8″
1″ squares

SPOON HOLDERS
3/8″ stock   1/2″ squares

BLADE DIVIDER

HANDLE TRAY

⅜ x ¾″ edge rabbet, both sides

Colonial cutlery cupboard

■ IF YOU'VE been looking for something a little out-of-the-ordinary to build, this version of an Early American cupboard can easily fill the bill. Though the one shown is constructed of spruce and finished with a fruitwood stain, you may prefer hardwood. It just means the project will cost slightly more to build. Either way, the cupboard will be a practical and beautiful addition to your home.

Before you start, decide exactly which cutlery you will want to store in the cupboard. Then you can alter dimensions before making any cuts. Equally important is the location of the knifeholders in the cupboard and drawers. Your inventory may vary somewhat from ours, so some adjustments may be necessary here, too. Use your favorite finish, but a tough, strong varnish is probably the best choice for both durability and appearance.

Built-ins for kitchen and laundry

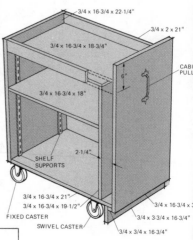

3/4 x 16-3/4 x 22-1/4"

3/4 x 2 x 21"

3/4 x 16-3/4 x 18-3/4"

CABI
PULL

6"

3/4 x 16-3/4 x 18"

2-1/4"

SHELF
SUPPORTS

3/4 x 16-3/4 x 21"
3/4 x 16-3/4 x 19-1/2"

FIXED CASTER

3/4 x 16-3/4 x 3

SWIVEL CASTER

3/4 x 3-3/4 x 16-3/4"

3/4 x 3/4 x 16-3/4"

ROLL-OUT appliance cart (left) poses as cabinet door when parked. Slide-out dish shelves are accessible from sides. Dishwasher (right), installed at counter level, requires no stooping to load and unload.

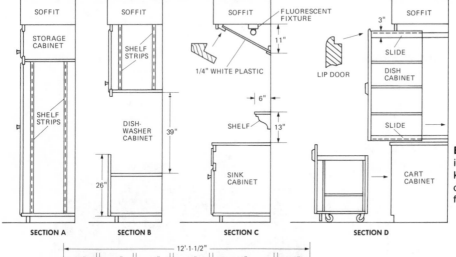

SOFFIT

STORAGE
CABINET

SHELF
STRIPS

SECTION A

SOFFIT

SHELF
STRIPS

DISH-
WASHER
CABINET

39"

26"

SECTION B

SOFFIT

FLUORESCENT
FIXTURE

11"

1/4" WHITE PLASTIC

6"

SHELF

13"

SINK
CABINET

SECTION C

LIP DOOR

3"

SOFFIT

SLIDE

DISH
CABINET

SLIDE

CART
CABINET

SECTION D

ELEVATION and section drawings at left show how one-wall kitchen is built. Plywood forms compartments; edges are faced with 1 x 2s.

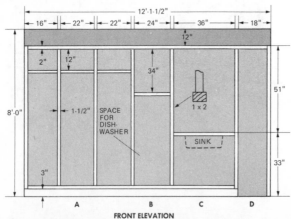

12'-1-1/2"

16"   22"   22"   24"   36"   18"

12"

2"   12"

34"

1-1/2"

SPACE
FOR
DISH-
WASHER

1 x 2

SINK

51"

8'-0"

33"

3"

A   B   C   D

FRONT ELEVATION

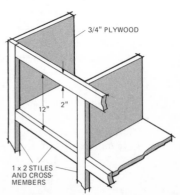

3/4" PLYWOOD

12"   2"

1 x 2 STILES
AND CROSS-
MEMBERS

■ STORAGE IS NEARLY as important as good equipment in creating an efficient laundry area. In this laundry center, cabinets to the left of the washer are fitted with pull-out wire-basket drawers to store soiled clothes according to wash loads. With four such drawers, it's easy to sort whites, colored, wash-and-wears and delicates. The cabinets to the right of the dryer provide cedar-lined storage for off-season clothes. Upper cabinets are used to safely store laundry aids out of reach of children.

Unusual aspects of the custom-designed kitchen, far left, include a no-stoop dishwasher that's 18 in. off the floor, and a roll-around appliance cart that pulls out of the cabinet convenient to a dinette table. It has a warming tray on top and adjustable shelves to keep small appliances extra handy.

Dish storage is made convenient in a pull-out cabinet above the appliance cart, and the sink located between washer and storage is made bright as day by an overhead fluorescent "skylight."

OVERHEAD shelf 12 in. from ceiling simplifies wiring of hanging lights and offers useful storage space.

SINK IS CONVENIENT to dishwasher and open-sided pull-out dish cabinet. Shelf over sink is for accessories; white plastic "skylight" conceals fluorescent fixture. Sink area is lined with matching room paneling. Appliance cart parks in compartment below dish storage, looks like matching cabinet door.

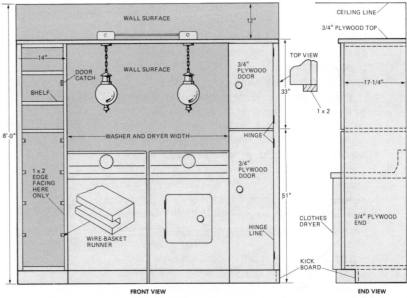

FRONT VIEW

END VIEW

Hideaways for kitchen and laundry

■ A MUD ROOM need not look like a mud room. It can be the gay and colorful entry you see here. With shelves standing by to corral boots, lunch boxes, jump ropes and baseball gear, the family back-door entry takes on anything but the look of a corner catch-all. When the shelves are painted lively colors to tie in with matching colors on the entry door itself, the overall effect adds a touch of excitement.

There's nothing to making such a shelf unit. For maximum simplicity, the whole thing, except for the back, is made from stock 1 x 10 boards which you just saw to length. If rabbets pose a problem to cut, forget them and let the plywood back lap the rear edges. The jigsawed letters can be the youngsters' initials.

When a convertible dishwasher can join in and be a part of a cooking/serving center, it's almost better than having a built-in unit, even when there is room for one. In this case there wasn't, but there was still the question of where to park a convertible out of sight when not in use. The answer was the clever side-by-side storage unit, shown above, which provides not only the perfect hideaway for a convertible dishwasher but also lots of storage for small appliances and bulky serving dishes as well. What's more, the top of the hideaway lifts up to reveal a handy wood cutting block perched on top of the dishwasher. When it's completely closed, no one would ever guess there's a dishwasher parked inside.

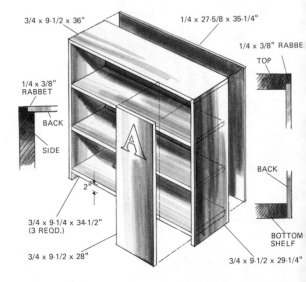

3/4 x 9-1/2 x 36"

1/4 x 27-5/8 x 35-1/4"

1/4 x 3/8" RABBE

TOP

1/4 x 3/8" RABBET

BACK

SIDE

BACK

2"

3/4 x 9-1/4 x 34-1/2" (3 REQD.)

3/4 x 9-1/2 x 28"

BOTTOM SHELF

3/4 x 9-1/2 x 29-1/4"

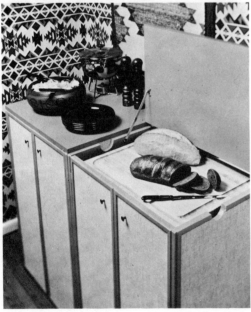

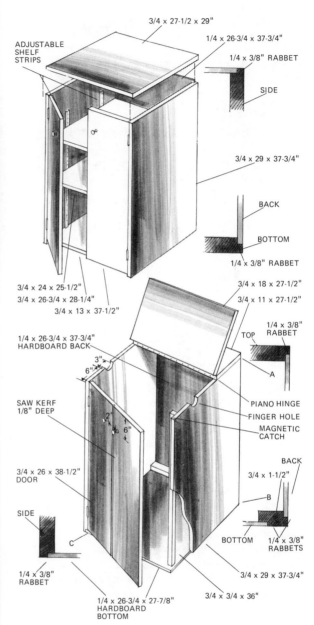

The twin cabinets have wipe-clean plastic-laminate tops and sides covered with natural grass-cloth vinyl accented with screen molding painted bright orange to match countertops.

Both boxlike cabinets are identical in overall size. Except for the ¼-in. hardboard bottom of the washer cabinet and the backs of both, ¾-in. plywood is used throughout. The joinery can be simplified where the work is being done primarily with hammer and saw. Rabbet joints add to overall sturdiness and offer no problem when you have a table saw. However, the backs can be merely lapped and nailed. The washer cabinet has a single door made to look like double doors by running a saw kerf down the middle.

Build a hood for an over-oven range

■ AFTER YOU ADD a wall oven over a kitchen range, you may not be able to find a hood with an exhaust fan that is going to fit between the cabinets. Commercial hoods may be either too wide or too narrow. That's when you should decide to make your own—like this attractive Colonial hood, which fits the space in your kitchen between the soffit and the top of the oven and the two flanking cabinets.

Install an exhaust fan in the wall over the oven, venting it to the outside. Wire it to a conveniently located switch. In the one shown here, the switch is located under the cabinets. The fan not only exhausts the heat from the oven but also the cooking odors and grease-laden vapors from the range as well. Removable filters are used to trap the grease.

Form the hood from a 36×94-in. sheet of 30-ga. sheet metal, cutting it according to the pattern shown, with measurements to fit your space. Most of the bends are made 90° to form flanges. The exceptions are those along the bottom edges, which are bent 180° and hammered flat to stiffen the metal. You can use Pop rivets to join the sides to the top. A neat job of bending results from using two straight pieces of wood and clamping them to each side of the metal along the line of bend.

The built-up, 3-in.-wide wood trim along the sides and front of the hood is made in one piece as shown in detail **A**, then mitered at the corners to fit. The corner trim pieces are preassembled in a similar way, then cut to fit and attached to the hood with sheet metal screws. Rivet 1×1-in. metal angles to the bottom hood flanges to hold removable grease filters. The corner strips, as well as the strips applied to the face of the hood, not only add decoration but actually serve to stiffen the hood.

The finished hood can be spray-painted a complementary color, or covered with the same wallpaper pattern you use in the rest of the kitchen. It would be best to apply the paper before adding the decorative wood strips. For a bit of Early American decor, you can add a brass eagle, as shown here.

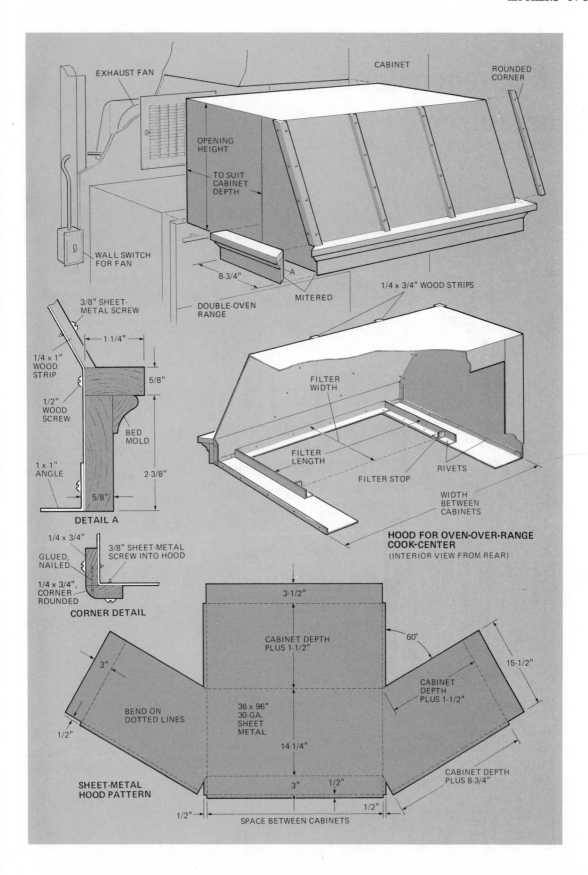

EXHAUST FAN

CABINET

ROUNDED CORNER

OPENING HEIGHT

TO SUIT CABINET DEPTH

WALL SWITCH FOR FAN

8-3/4"

A

MITERED

DOUBLE-OVEN RANGE

1/4 x 3/4" WOOD STRIPS

DETAIL A

3/8" SHEET-METAL SCREW

1/4 x 1" WOOD STRIP

1/2" WOOD SCREW

1 x 1" ANGLE

1-1/4"

5/8"

BED MOLD

2-3/8"

5/8"

CORNER DETAIL

1/4 x 3/4"

GLUED, NAILED

1/4 x 3/4", CORNER ROUNDED

3/8" SHEET-METAL SCREW INTO HOOD

FILTER WIDTH

FILTER LENGTH

FILTER STOP

RIVETS

WIDTH BETWEEN CABINETS

HOOD FOR OVEN-OVER-RANGE COOK-CENTER
(INTERIOR VIEW FROM REAR)

SHEET-METAL HOOD PATTERN

3-1/2"

CABINET DEPTH PLUS 1-1/2"

60°

15-1/2"

3"

CABINET DEPTH PLUS 1-1/2"

BEND ON DOTTED LINES

36 x 96" 30-GA. SHEET METAL

14-1/4"

1/2"

CABINET DEPTH PLUS 8-3/4"

3"

1/2"

1/2"

1/2"

SPACE BETWEEN CABINETS

Kitchen door organizer

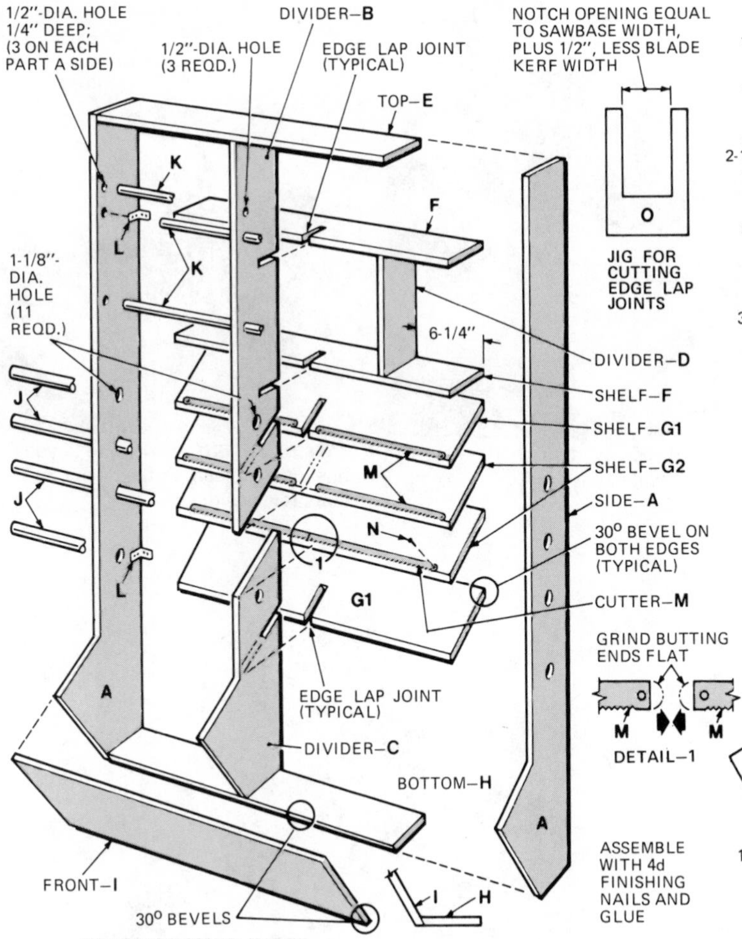
1/2"-DIA. HOLE 1/4" DEEP; (3 ON EACH PART A SIDE)
DIVIDER–B
1/2"-DIA. HOLE (3 REQD.)
EDGE LAP JOINT (TYPICAL)
TOP–E
NOTCH OPENING EQUAL TO SAWBASE WIDTH, PLUS 1/2", LESS BLADE KERF WIDTH
O
JIG FOR CUTTING EDGE LAP JOINTS
K
F
L
K
1-1/8"-DIA. HOLE (11 REQD.)
6-1/4"
J
J
DIVIDER–D
SHELF–F
SHELF–G1
SHELF–G2
M
SIDE–A
N
30° BEVEL ON BOTH EDGES (TYPICAL)
1
G1
CUTTER–M
L
GRIND BUTTING ENDS FLAT
A
EDGE LAP JOINT (TYPICAL)
M
M
DETAIL–1
DIVIDER–C
BOTTOM–H
A
ASSEMBLE WITH 4d FINISHING NAILS AND GLUE
FRONT–I
I
H
30° BEVELS
EXPLODED ASSEMBLY VIEW

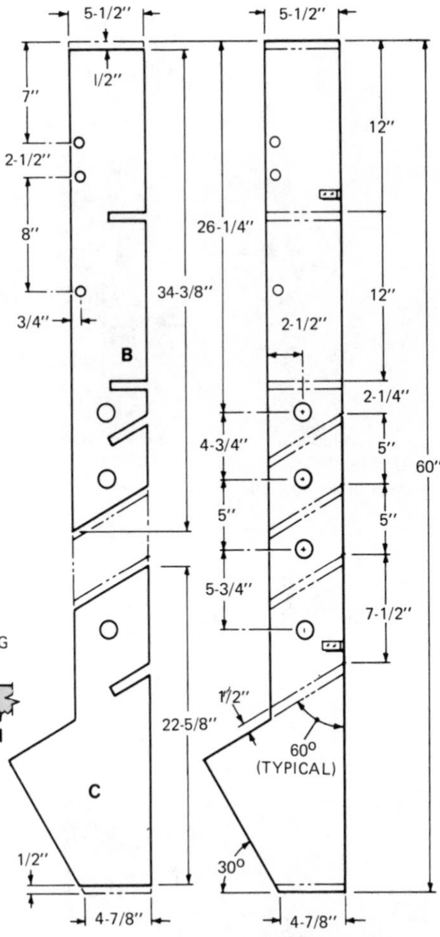
5-1/2"
1/2"
7"
2-1/2"
8"
3/4"
34-3/8"
B
22-5/8"
C
1/2"
4-7/8"
5-1/2"
12"
26-1/4"
12"
2-1/2"
2-1/4"
4-3/4"
5"
60"
5"
5"
5-3/4"
7-1/2"
1/2"
60° (TYPICAL)
30°
4-7/8"
DIVIDERS B AND C

SIDE A

■ MAKE THIS KITCHEN organizer and you'll find the whole family enjoying its conveniences. You can install it on the back of any door, such as the one leading to the basement, garage or pantry. It is so attractive, though, you may not want to hide it.

The unit has received careful consideration for storing the most commonly used kitchen items. Toxic liquids are stored on the upper shelves out of reach of children; lower bins may contain paper cups, napkins and anything else children use regularly.

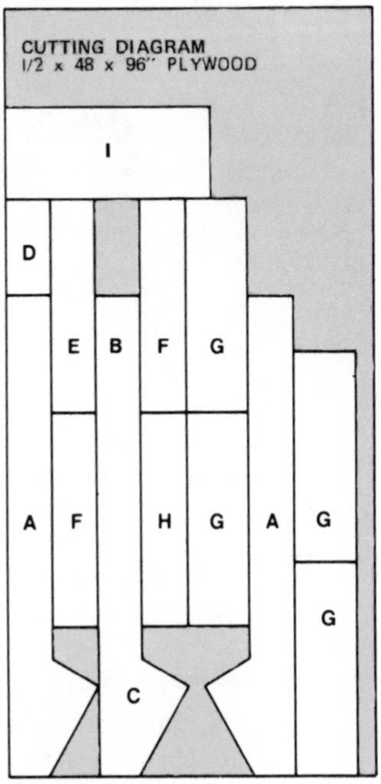
CUTTING DIAGRAM
1/2 x 48 x 96" PLYWOOD
I
D
E
B
F
G
A
F
H
G
A
G
G
C

MATERIALS LIST—KITCHEN ORGANIZER

Key	No.	Size and description (use)
A	2	½ x 10⅜ x 60" plywood (side)
B	1	½ x 3½ x 34⅜" (approx.) plywood (divider)
C	1	½ x 10⅜ x 22⅝" (approx.) plywood (divider)
D	1	½ x 5½ x 11½" plywood (divider)
E	1	½ x 5½ x 26½" plywood (top)
F	2	½ x 5½ x 26½" plywood (shelf)
G	4	½ x 6⅝ (approx.) x 26½" plywood (shelf)
H	1	½ x 5½ x 26½" plywood (bottom)
I	1	½ x 11 x 27½" plywood (front)
J	4	1"-dia. x 31" dowel
K	3	½"-dia. x 27" dowel
L	4	1½" corner brace with eight ½" No. 6 fh screws
M	6	12" hacksaw blade
N		½" No. 6 rh screw (as reqd.)
O	1	¼" x 8 x 12" hardboard or plywood (jig)

Misc.: Carpenter's glue, paint, sandpaper.

MAKE LOWER, angled cuts of sides with circular saw and guide strip.

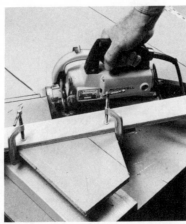

RESET GUIDE, even for short cuts, each time you make a cut.

ALWAYS EXTEND guide strip beyond edge of workpiece. Cutting diagram allows removal of waste.

SECURE CUTTING jig to workpiece, using hand-screw or C-clamp. Make opening in jig long enough to cut both 60° and 90° slots.

SHOWN HERE READY for assembly are parts of the kitchen organizer cut from one 4x8 plywood panel. Use MDO (medium density overlaid) plywood for best results.

Perhaps the neatest features are the wrapping dispensers. Hacksaw blades serve as cutting edges for aluminum foil and the like and make the dispensing of these materials a fast, one-hand operation. You can also see when you're getting low on wraps, as the rolls are not concealed in awkward boxes.

Materials used

The unit is constructed of ½-in. MDO (medium density overlaid) plywood. Having a very smooth surface, this is more costly than ordinary fir plywood, but it is well worth the difference for several other advantages. It is made with good-quality inner plies and thus there are no large voids or splintery areas. An MDO panel does not warp easily and doesn't splinter at the edge when sawed. Its smooth, flat surface is especially well suited for painting.

Cutting plan

All required pieces can be cut from one 4x8 panel if you follow the cutting plan shown. The initial cuts can be made with a sabre saw or cir-

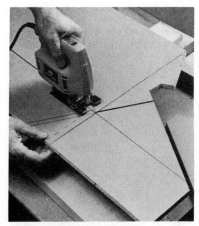

COMPLETE CIRCULAR SAW cuts with sabre saw. Cut slowly with steady hand or use a straightedge positioned to give clean line.

SANDWICH-CLAMP three vertical members together (before centerpiece is cut). Sand exposed edges with 120-grit, then 150-grit paper.

USE DRILL press or portable guide to assure boring holes straight. Place workpiece on scrap for a clean hole. Pilot holes make job easier.

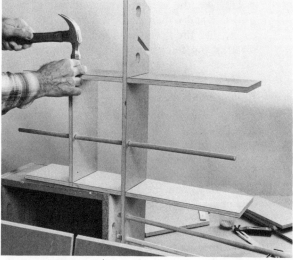

TEMPORARY CLEATS are tack-nailed below each shelf location to simplify assembly.

EVEN DULL hacksaw blades will work well as cutting edges for the various wrappings.

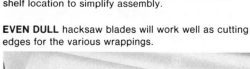

BEGIN ASSEMBLING shelves and dividers. The small divider must be placed in position with dowel before attaching end.

AFTER ALL PARTS are attached to center divider, including dowels, sides are easily added using nails and carpenter's glue, with cabinet turned on its side as shown.

cular saw. Whatever saw you use, be sure to use a smooth-cutting plywood blade and set up your guides carefully so that you will have finished cuts in one step. Remember to allow for the saw kerf when you lay out the cutting pattern.

A 4x8 panel can be cumbersome to work with, so always have it properly supported for its entire length. Readjust your supports after each cut and avoid a situation in which it will be awkward to make the full length of the cut in one run.

Make the first cut across the panel to yield the piece from which the front (I) is cut. This procedure will allow you to make several lengthwise cuts to get smaller sections that are easier to handle. Next, use clamps and a straight strip of wood as a guide to make the angled cuts for the sides. Cut to within 1 in. of the inside corners with the circular saw, then use the sabre saw to finish the corner cuts.

Although the center divider consists of two pieces (B and C) initially, cut it as a single unit exactly like the two sides. Then clamp all three together and finish-sand the edges that will be exposed.

Boring the dowel holes

Mark center points for the 1⅛-in.-diameter dowel holes on one side of the sandwiched pieces. Use a 1⅛-in. spade bit and be sure to back up the work with a wood block to prevent tearing as the bit breaks through. Since good alignment of the holes is important, use a guide with your portable drill or use a drill press.

Before separating the three pieces, mark off the measurements for the shelves on both sides. Join these respective marks across the edges, front and back, with a straight pencil line.

Now, separate the sides and centerpiece and mark the center points for the ½-in.-diameter dowel holes in the centerpiece. Note that the holes for the small dowels are bored through the centerpiece, but are bored only ¼ in. deep in the inside surface of each sidepiece. This requires the use of a twist drill with a bit stop.

After the holes have been bored in the centerpiece, connect the marks on the front and back edges to produce the 60° and 90° angle lines. Cut piece B-C into the two dividers, B and C.

The angled shelves are cut to size with a 30° bevel on the front and back edges. A table saw is ideal for these cuts, but they can be made as well with a guide and a portable circular saw.

A jig for edge-lap joints

Edge-lap joints are used to attach the shelves to the center dividers. These are cut with a sabre saw and a simple jig.

To make the jig, cut a piece of ¼-in. plywood or hardboard to 8x12 in. To determine the width of the slot in the jig, measure the width of the saw base and add ½ in. (thickness of the stock). Then subtract the kerf (thickness of the saw blade).

The length of the slot should be more than 3⁵⁄₁₆ in. (half of the angled shelf width before bevels), plus the distance from the front edge of the sabre-saw shoe. Cut the slots before you make the bevels. Note that the slots in shelves F should be exactly half the width of the shelf and the divider (B) or 2¾ in., as these joints are both positioned at right angles.

Before using the jig on a workpiece, make test cuts in scrap to check the fit of the joint produced. The parts should fit together easily without gaps.

Assembling the organizer

Attach the two upper shelves to the center divider and nail in the short vertical divider (D). Insert the ½-in. dowels.

The shelves will automatically be positioned on the center dividers, but you should use temporary cleats tacked to the sides in order to obtain an easy, accurate assembly of the sides to the shelves. Tack cleats to the sides with finishing nails. Leave the heads protruding so the cleats can be removed easily after assembly.

Use carpenter's glue and 1½-in. (4d) finishing nails on all butt joints. If you bore small pilot holes for the nails in the sides in advance, you'll have an easier time getting them in line and centered. Attach the front panel last.

Now, set all nailheads and cover them with a wood filler. Finish-sand with 120-grit paper and round over all edges slightly.

Positioning the blades

Buy inexpensive hacksaw blades or use old ones. Use ½-in. No. 6 roundhead screws to attach them to the shelves. Position the blades so that the serrated edges overhang the shelf by about ⅛-in. If you grind the rounded ends square, the cutting edges of abutting blades will be continuous for a nice finishing touch.

Attach four 1½-in. corner irons flush with the back to permit hanging.

TIP-OUT BIN fully open. The front compartment stores long kitchen tools. A hole provides access to rags.

HALF-OPEN POSITION. Bin sides are hardboard painted with epoxy enamel. The front is faced with sheet metal.

Kitchen space saver

■ WHAT DO YOU DO when a new stove turns out to be 6 in. narrower than the old one and leaves a gap too small for drawer or cabinet? One solution is to fill the space with a tip-out bin and add a longer counter-top.

Use the extra space to store kitchen tools that are too long to fit in conventional drawers. There is also a hole in the side for easy access to a hidden compartment.

As you see in the drawing, the bin was made pie-shape for balance. The shifting center of gravity will hold the bin fully open as shown above left, halfway open as shown above right, and fully closed. The dotted lines show where to form hidden storage compartments in the bin, with front space being accessible from one side. The back compartment makes a dandy place to keep rags, which can be grabbed through the hand hole in the side. The bin itself is hinged to a 2×4 toeboard that is painted to match the toeboard on adjoining cabinets.

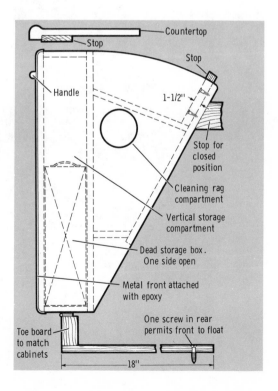

Countertop
Stop
Stop
Handle
1-1/2"
Stop for closed position
Cleaning rag compartment
Vertical storage compartment
Dead storage box. One side open
Metal front attached with epoxy
One screw in rear permits front to float
Toe board to match cabinets
18"

Mobile kitchen island rolls where you want it

■ KITCHEN ISLANDS have long been design favorites of people fortunate enough to have large kitchens. Such cabinets provide additional storage and counter space at the center of the room, while serving as an impromptu gathering area for socializing with family or house guests.

Now we've taken this good idea and made it better. We have created a movable kitchen island that adapts quickly to suit work and decorating needs. Because all three cabinet sections are castermounted and connected with hinges, several different configurations, as well as room positions, are possible. The unit includes space for knives, flatware, paper and canned goods,

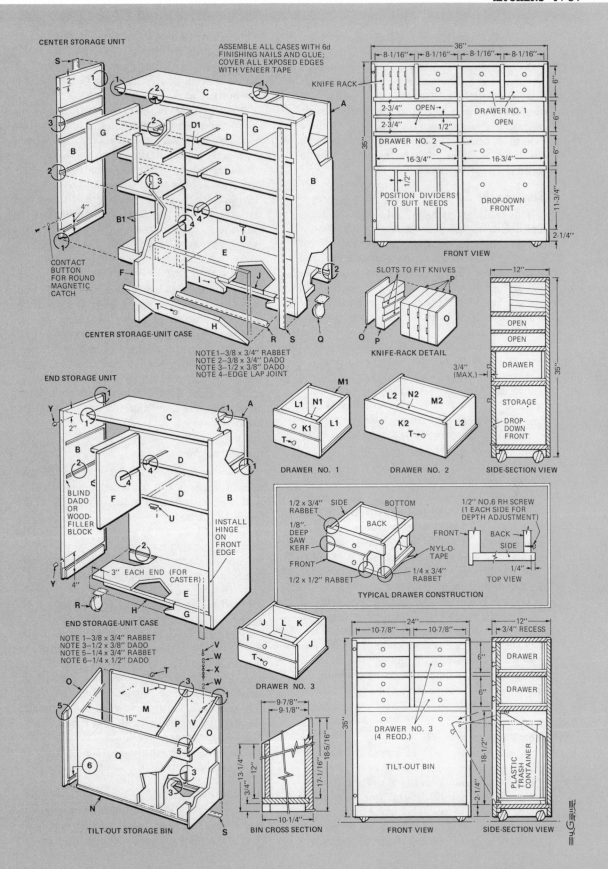

CENTER STORAGE UNIT

ASSEMBLE ALL CASES WITH 6d FINISHING NAILS AND GLUE; COVER ALL EXPOSED EDGES WITH VENEER TAPE

KNIFE RACK

CONTACT BUTTON FOR ROUND MAGNETIC CATCH

CENTER STORAGE-UNIT CASE

NOTE 1–3/8 × 3/4" RABBET
NOTE 2–3/8 × 3/4" DADO
NOTE 3–1/2 × 3/8" DADO
NOTE 4–EDGE LAP JOINT

FRONT VIEW

36"
8-1/16" 8-1/16" 8-1/16" 8-1/16"
6"
2-3/4" OPEN
DRAWER NO. 1 OPEN
2-3/4" 1/2"
6"
35"
DRAWER NO. 2
16-3/4" 16-3/4"
6"
POSITION DIVIDERS TO SUIT NEEDS
1/2"
DROP-DOWN FRONT
11-3/4"
2-1/4"

SLOTS TO FIT KNIVES
P
O
O P
KNIFE-RACK DETAIL

3/4" (MAX.)
12"
OPEN
OPEN
DRAWER
35"
STORAGE
DROP-DOWN FRONT
SIDE-SECTION VIEW

DRAWER NO. 1
M1
L1 N1
K1
L1

DRAWER NO. 2
L2 N2 M2
K2
L2

END STORAGE UNIT

BLIND DADO OR WOOD-FILLER BLOCK

INSTALL HINGE ON FRONT EDGE

END STORAGE-UNIT CASE

NOTE 1–3/8 × 3/4" RABBET
NOTE 3–1/2 × 3/8" DADO
NOTE 5–1/4 × 3/4" RABBET
NOTE 6–1/4 × 1/2" DADO

3" EACH END (FOR CASTER)

1/2 × 3/4" SIDE RABBET
1/8"-DEEP SAW KERF
FRONT
1/2 × 1/2" RABBET
SIDE
BOTTOM
BACK
1/4 × 3/4" RABBET
NYL-O-TAPE

1/2" NO.6 RH SCREW (1 EACH SIDE FOR DEPTH ADJUSTMENT)
FRONT BACK SIDE
1/4"
TOP VIEW

TYPICAL DRAWER CONSTRUCTION

DRAWER NO. 3
J L K
I J
T

TILT-OUT STORAGE BIN

V
W
X
W

BIN CROSS SECTION
9-7/8"
9-1/8"
13-1/4" 12"
18-5/16"
17-1/16"
3/4"
2-1/4"
10-1/4"

FRONT VIEW
24"
10-7/8" 10-7/8"
6"
6"
35"
DRAWER NO. 3 (4 REQD.)
TILT-OUT BIN

SIDE-SECTION VIEW
12"
3/4" RECESS
DRAWER
DRAWER
18-1/2"
2-1/4"
PLASTIC TRASH CONTAINER

plus a unique bar cabinet that lets you corral ice, glasses and spirits in one spot.

Complete plans and how-to-build instructions are presented on the following pages. Materials lists for all three units are provided. Study them carefully. You may be able to save yourself some expense if you purchase the wood for all three units at the same time. It's a good idea to have all parts and materials on hand before you begin construction of the island.

Starting the job

Before cutting anything, study all of the drawings carefully. There is nothing terribly sophisticated about the woodworking techniques employed here, but there are many details that you must observe. The layout of all the dadoes, rabbets and half-lapped joints must be precise, otherwise, the cabinet could be assembled out of square. If that happens, it will never open and close properly.

It's best to use plywood that is good on both sides (A-A) for this project, because many of the parts are visible from both sides. If the additional cost of this grade is prohibitive, use stock that's good on one side only (A-D) and fill all surface voids on the poor side. Also, try to construct the cases so that the poorer (D) surfaces face down or in.

Center storage unit

To build the center storage unit, cut the top, back, bottom, sides, shelves and dividers to size. Then lay out all the rabbets, dadoes and half-lapped joints shown in the drawing. Next, glue and nail together the sides, top and back, then install the bottom, toe kick (I) and support cleat (J). Check the cabinet for square.

If you've been careful cutting the parts to size—especially the back—the cabinet should be square and no adjustment will be necessary. However, if the case is slightly out of square, you must force (i.e., wrack) it until it's square and hold it that way with tacked-on braces until the glue dries. Leave the squared and braced cabinet clamped overnight.

Tape sides of drawers

Preassemble the knife rack and drawers as shown, then insert them into the case. The self-sticking nylon tape on each side of the drawer bottom assures that the drawers will slide easily without drawer guides. This nylon tape is approximately $\frac{1}{32}$ in. thick and is used on all the drawers in both the end and center storage units.

It also allows minor adjustments in the up and down position of the drawer, relative to the drawer opening. If your drawer is slightly out of square, place a double thickness of tape on the appropriate side.

The stop points of the drawers can also be adjusted. Simply turn the depth-adjustment screws on the back of each drawer until the drawer front is properly aligned in the closed position.

Cut the drop-down front panel to size and attach it to the top edge of the toe kick using a continuous hinge. Install the magnetic catch and contact plate for this door, then finish-sand the entire unit, ending up with 150-grit sandpaper. Remove the dust with a brush and tack cloth.

End storage unit

There is one major difference between the end storage unit and the center unit, which can be seen on the side-section view: The drawers and the tilt-out bin on the end unit are recessed ¾ in. from the front edge of the cabinet case. This recess is needed to provide clearance for the drawer and bin pulls when the two units are closed together. Because of this, be sure to use pulls which project no more than ¾ in. from the drawer and bin fronts.

Cut the dadoes

Also note the blind shelf dadoes on the case sides of this unit. Cut these with a dado head in your table saw or with a router using either of the following methods:
• Plow the dado all the way across the side and then glue in a small filler block.
• Stop the dado just short of the appropriate point and clean out the curved corners with a sharp chisel.

Install the shelves and divider and let the assembly dry overnight.

Before cutting the parts for the tilt-out bin, measure the case opening and make dimension adjustments if necessary. Test-fit the bin front with the hinge installed; when satisfied with fit, remove the front and assemble the entire bin with glue and nails. Let the assembly dry overnight.

Install the magnetic catch and contact plate. Then assemble and install the drawers as described earlier. Attach the restraining-chain assembly and finish-sand the whole unit.

Bar cabinet

Assemble the bar cabinet in the same manner as the other units and attach the shelf standards (BB) to the sides and the lower compartment di-

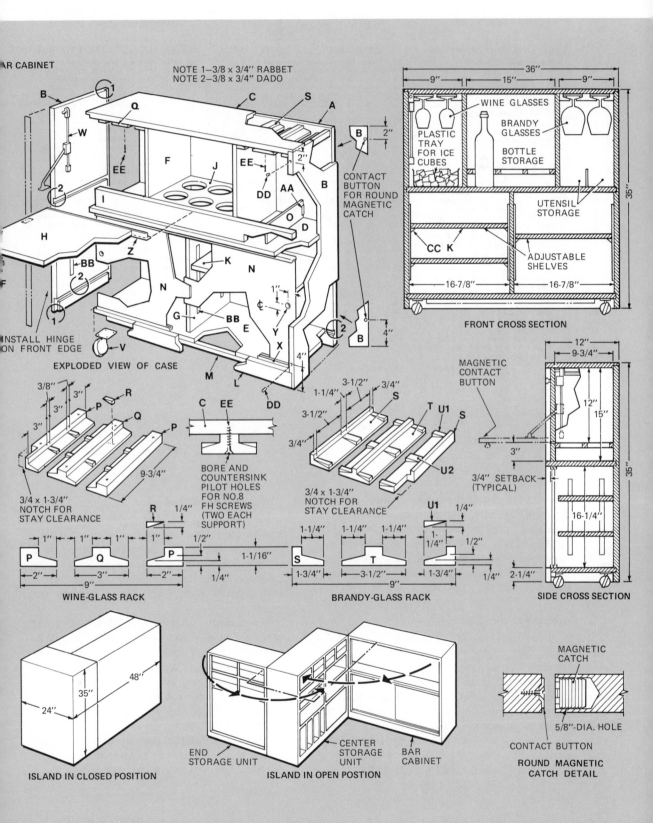

AR CABINET

NOTE 1–3/8 x 3/4″ RABBET
NOTE 2–3/8 x 3/4″ DADO

CONTACT BUTTON FOR ROUND MAGNETIC CATCH

INSTALL HINGE ON FRONT EDGE

EXPLODED VIEW OF CASE

WINE GLASSES
BRANDY GLASSES
BOTTLE STORAGE
PLASTIC TRAY FOR ICE CUBES
UTENSIL STORAGE
CC K
ADJUSTABLE SHELVES
16-7/8″   16-7/8″

FRONT CROSS SECTION

3/4 x 1-3/4″ NOTCH FOR STAY CLEARANCE

BORE AND COUNTERSINK PILOT HOLES FOR NO.8 FH SCREWS (TWO EACH SUPPORT)

3/4 x 1-3/4″ NOTCH FOR STAY CLEARANCE

WINE-GLASS RACK

BRANDY-GLASS RACK

MAGNETIC CONTACT BUTTON

3/4″ SETBACK (TYPICAL)

16-1/4″

SIDE CROSS SECTION

ISLAND IN CLOSED POSITION

END STORAGE UNIT
CENTER STORAGE UNIT
BAR CABINET

ISLAND IN OPEN POSTION

MAGNETIC CATCH
5/8″-DIA. HOLE
CONTACT BUTTON

ROUND MAGNETIC CATCH DETAIL

MATERIALS LIST—BAR CABINET UNIT

Key	No.	Size and description (use)
A	1	3/4 × 345/8 × 351/4" plywood (back)
B	2	3/4 × 12 × 345/8" plywood (side)
C	1	3/4 × 12 × 36" plywood (top)
D	1	3/4 × 115/8 × 351/4" plywood (shelf)
E	1	3/4 × 107/8 × 351/4" plywood (bottom)
F	2	3/4 × 93/4 × 15" plywood (top divider)
G	1	3/4 × 91/2 × 16⅜ plywood (bottom divider)
H	1	3/4 × 1113/16 × 343/8" plywood (door)
I	1	3/4 × 3 × 341/2" plywood (rail)
J	1	3/4 × 93/4 × 15" plywood (bottle shelf)
K	3	3/4 × 91/2 × 163/8" plywood (adjustable shelf)
L	1	3/4 × 21/4 × 351/4" plywood (toe kick)
M	1	3/4 × 3/4 × 30" pine (cleat)
N	2	1/4 × 1513/16 × 173/4" plywood (sliding door)
O	1	1/4 × 3 × 95/8" plywood (divider)
P	2	11/16 × 2 × 93/4" pine (end support)
Q	1	11/16 × 3 × 93/4" pine (center support)
R	8	1/4 × 3/8 × 1" pine lattice (glass divider)
S	2	11/16 × 13/4 × 93/4" pine (end support)
T	1	11/16 × 31/2 × 93/4" pine (center support)
U1	8	1/4 × 3/4 × 11/4" pine lattice (glass divider)
U2	4	1/4 × 11/4 × 351/4" pine lattice (glass divider)
V*	4	21/2" flat plate ball caster
W**	2	flap stay
X		Plastic track for overlapping 1/4" doors
Y	2	1"-dia. finger pull
Z	1	11/2 × 341/4" continuous hinge
AA**	2	zip clip
BB	8	12" shelf standard
CC	12	Shelf clips
DD**	2	round magnetic catch
EE	12	11/2" No. 8 fh screws
FF	2	3/4"-dia. × 3/4"-long porcelain knob

Misc.: 6d finishing nails, glue, veneer tape.

MATERIALS LIST—CENTER UNIT

Key	No.	Size and description (use)
A	1	3/4 × 345/8 × 351/4" plywood (back)
B	2	3/4 × 12 × 345/8" plywood (side)
B1	3	1/2 × 111/4 × 113/4" plywood (divider)
C	1	3/4 × 12 × 36" plywood (top)
D	3	3/4 × 111/4 × 351/4" plywood (shelf)
D1	1	1/2 × 111/4 × 175/8" plywood (shelf)
E	1	3/4 × 107/8 × 351/4" plywood (bottom)
F	1	3/4 × 111/4 × 32" plywood (divider)
G	2	3/4 × 63/4 × 111/4" plywood (divider)
H	1	3/4 × 119/16 × 163/4" plywood (door)
I	1	3/4 × 21/4 × 351/4" plywood (toe kick)
J	1	3/4 × 3/4 × 30" pine (cleat)
DRAWER No. 1		
K1	3	3/4 × 57/8 × 715/16" plywood (front)
L1	6	1/2 × 55/8 × 103/4" plywood (side)
M1	3	1/2 × 53/8 × 67/16" plywood (back)
N1	3	1/2 × 715/16 × 103/4" plywood (bottom)
DRAWER No. 2		
K2	2	3/4 × 57/8 × 163/4" plywood (front)
L2	4	1/2 × 55/8 × 103/4" plywood (side)
M2	2	1/2 × 53/8 × 151/4" plywood (back)
N2	2	1/2 × 103/4 × 163/4" plywood (bottom)
KNIFE RACK		
O	2	1/4 × 6 × 71/4" pine (filler block)
P	5	11/2 × 6 × 71/4" fir (notched block)
HARDWARE		
Q*	4	21/2" flat plate ball caster
R	1	11/2 × 165/8" continuous hinge
S	2	11/2 × 35" continuous hinge
T	12	3/4"-dia. × 3/4"-long porcelain knob
U	1	Magnetic catch with strike

Misc.: 6d finishing nails, glue, veneer tape.

MATERIALS LIST—END STORAGE UNIT

Key	No.	Size and description (use)
A	1	3/4 × 231/4 × 345/8" plywood (back)
B	2	3/4 × 12 × 345/8" plywood (side)
C	1	3/4 × 12 × 24" plywood (top)
D	2	3/4 × 101/2 × 231/4" plywood (shelf)
E	1	3/4 × 107/8 × 231/4" plywood (bottom)
F	1	3/4 × 101/2 × 123/4" plywood (divider)
G	1	3/4 × 21/4 × 231/4" plywood (toe kick)
H	1	3/4 × 3/4 × 18" pine (cleat)
DRAWER No. 3		
I	4	3/4 × 57/8 × 103/4" plywood (front)
J	8	1/2 × 55/8 × 10" plywood (side)
K	4	1/2 × 53/8 × 91/4" plywood (back)
L	4	1/2 × 10 × 103/4" plywood (bottom)
TILT-OUT BIN		
M	1	3/4 × 185/16 × 223/8" plywood (front)
N	1	1/2 × 97/8 × 213/8" plywood (bottom)
O	2	1/2 × 23/8 × 185/16" plywood (side)
P	1	1/2 × 91/8 × 171/16" plywood (divider)
Q	1	1/2 × 12 × 213/8" plywood (back)
HARDWARE		
R*	4	21/2" flat plate ball caster No. 9360
S	1	11/2 × 221/4" continuous hinge
T	10	3/4"-dia. × 3/4"-long porcelain knob
U	1	Magnetic catch with strike
V	2	Screw eye
W	2	S-hook
X		12" chain (cut to length)
Y**	2	round magnetic catch

Misc.: 6d finishing nails, glue, veneer tape.

vider. Next, install the upper dividers and the bottle storage rack, and fabricate and install the two glass racks as shown in the drawing. The wedge-shaped cleats on these racks were designed to prevent the glasses from hitting each other when the island is opened, closed or being rolled around the room.

Complete the assembly

Install the plywood rail (I) and the utensil divider, then cut the drop-down door to size and attach it with a continuous hinge. Add both stays (W) for this door and the magnetic catch plates. Then install the sliding-door tracks and doors for the lower compartment; bore the holes for the finger pulls. Don't install the pulls yet; wait until after the case has been painted. Apply the veneer tape to the exposed edges, finish-sand the entire unit, then dust and wipe with a tack cloth.

Paint and hardware

Before priming and painting the cases, position and bore the holes for the four round magnetic catches as shown. These serve to hold the three units together in the closed position. Remove the catches and their corresponding contact buttons and reinstall them after you've finished the painting.

Temporarily install the continuous hinges that join the cabinet units to make certain the units fit as they should. At this time, you should also install the casters to check the unit for roll.

When you're satisfied that all the carpentry is satisfactory, remove the cabinet-joining hinges and cover the casters with masking tape, then paint.

After the paint dries, the units can be reassembled with the continuous hinges and the protective tape can be removed from the casters.

Storage space in your kitchen

■ TURN THE HIGH-TRAFFIC ROOM of your home, the kitchen, into a comfortable, livable and highly efficient area—simply by incorporating just a few of these storage ideas in it or by building in two or three of these worksavers.

What's more, they're all uncomplicated enough to be tackled one or two at a time each winter weekend so that by the time spring rolls around, the dollar value and convenience of your home will have increased considerably.

One such convenience feature is the storage area for rolled tablecloths, while another is a pair of simple drawers used exclusively for pans and trays that are too awkward to store in a conventional fashion.

The island unit has a triple sink and stainless steel top; it could be installed easily in the wasted space in the center of an average kitchen. It also offers the bonus feature of providing enough under-the-sink space to hold trash cans and cleaning supplies. A pull-out shelf rests hidden in the island until needed, while a separate, but nevertheless handy, cutting board is similarly built in next to the sink.

The cabinets around the perimeter of the 12×14-ft. kitchen also were designed with livabil-

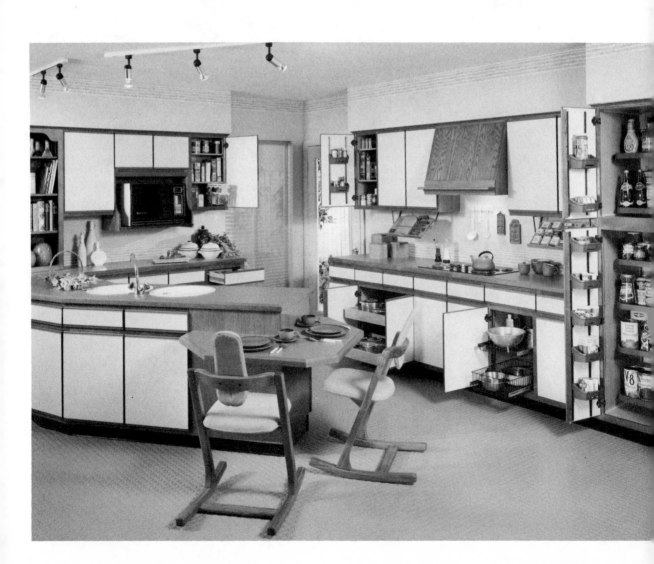

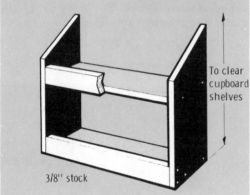

SMALL BOTTLES of spices can be neatly arranged in a simple rack fitted to the inside of a door.

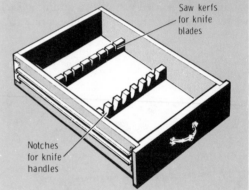

KNIFE DRAWER with two shaped cross members will stow knives out of sight and protect them from damage.

SIMPLE DRAWERS and pull-out rods can be used effectively to store pots and pans within your reach.

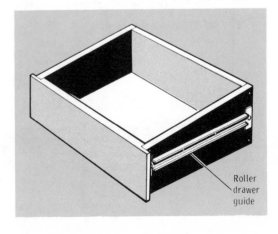

HANDY CUTTING surface is easy to build and install. It's basically just a bottomless drawer fitted with a top that will hold up under a knife blade.

ity in mind. With careful planning, you can transform a single 12-ft. wall into more than 300 ft. of shelving. To the right of the refrigerator, for example, four standard-size doors open to uncover a broom closet and shallow pantry-type storage. Three of the doors are lined with shelves, and three deep drawers at the bottom hold odd-sized containers, supplies and bottles.

In fact, there are drawers and shelves neatly tucked away in nearly every cabinet. In one, a linen drawer replaces the bottom shelf; in another, two drawers hold large pans and pan covers; while in a third, pull-out racks hold pans with handles in a vertical, spacesaving position. Thus, the spacemakers are also backsavers since it's possible to reach any item without resorting to kneeling or bending over for more than a few seconds.

In most kitchens, it's usually possible to find hidden or otherwise wasted space that could be put to effective use as a storage area. A careful study of the plans of your home likely will reveal space between the walls of additions, at the back of deep closets or around the stairways and built-in appliances.

Other special-use spacesavers that you could easily build into your kitchen take the forms of spice racks, knife drawers, bread bins and

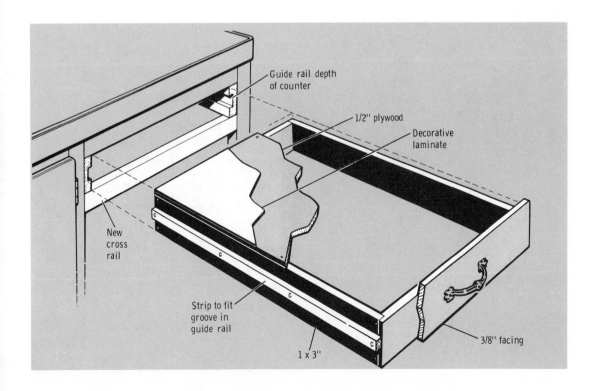

multi-shelf units used strictly for canned or bottled goods. Here again, the trick is to search out unused space and put it to work—preferably using it to solve the problem of storing awkward, bulky, shelf-robbing items such as toasters, mixers and similar appliances.

Combine these simple kitchen aids and worksavers with such conveniences as lighting fixtures concealed under the cabinets and adequate electrical outlets, and you'll find that your once-congested kitchen will be transformed into a highly organized, highly livable center.

Yet, as previously pointed out, you can make these additions and changes gradually and without great expense since you likely have enough odd pieces of lumber left over from old projects to complete five or six of these weekend projects at your leisure. Also noteworthy is the fact that it's not necessary to tear up the kitchen and disrupt its use during this modernization program.

ROLL-OUT BINS placed in the bottom of cabinets are for storage of kitchen towels and cleaning supplies. They eliminate kneeling to remove items in back.

PANTRY SHELVES built on doors can provide storage space that's ideal for canned and bottled supplies.

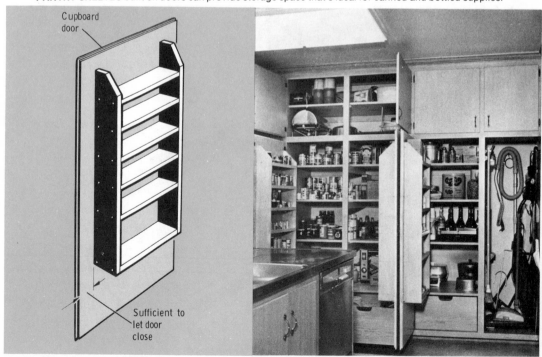

Cupboard door

Sufficient to let door close

Pantry on wheels

■ AFTER REPEATEDLY digging into a deep, dark pantry to retrieve a bottle of soy sauce or a can of tomato paste, you may want to look at these roll-out racks of shelves. The racks stand side by side and are mounted on rollers. When one of the racks is pulled out, all items on its shelves are visible and accessible.

The racks are easy-to-build, ¾-in. plywood frames, assembled using butt joints. Cleats at the joints serve as strengtheners. The ½-in. plywood shelves provide further rigidity.

The racks move on appliance rollers. These multiwheeled plastic or aluminum supports are used for moving refrigerators and stoves. You can purchase them at hardware and discount stores or by mail. You'll need one set for each rack.

You can roll out the racks easily with a brass pull, positioned slightly above waist height on the side of the rack facing out.

To assemble and finish the racks, you'll need a hammer, drill, screwdriver, nailset, paint brush and some 80- and 120-grit sandpaper. A corner clamp is also handy. Use the clamp at each shelf corner to hold the parts in place while you attach them with nails or screws.

To determine the number and size of racks your pantry can accommodate, measure the depth of the pantry or closet and the height and width of the opening. Allow ½ to 1 in. clearance at the sides and between racks. Racks at least 8 in. wide accept the rollers best, since both mates of a set can be extended to the same length. Subtract the height of the appliance rollers from the height of the opening to get the maximum height of the rack sides.

Next, decide upon the number of shelves you would like per rack. Either draw a rough sketch to scale for each rack, including the shelves, or use the dimensions on the drawing below, if your pantry can hold this size rack. From the drawing,

BEFORE BUILDING the pantry on wheels, the 30-in.-deep pantry was too cavernous to display its contents. You had to take everything off the front of a shelf to locate items pushed to the back.

NEARLY EVERY SIZE PACKAGE is visible and readily accessible in this pantry on wheels. Labeling each rack with its contents makes locating items even easier. On racks 8 in. or wider, appliance roller mates can be extended to the same length and fastened to a rack. On narrower racks, stagger rollers.

make a materials list you'll need when purchasing lumber and hardware.

Assembly and painting

Cut the parts to size, then sand them smooth, dusting with a clean brush between steps.

Lay out the rack sides. Prebore the cleats and, using a corner clamp, fasten them to the sides with glue and screws. Fasten the top and bottom pieces to the cleats with glue and nails. Then hammer finishing nails through the rack sides into the ends of the top and bottom. Set nails and fill holes with wood putty.

Prime and paint the shelves with a semigloss plastic or acrylic latex paint before installing. You can hang each shelf to dry by a string fastened to a small nail driven partway into one end. Then prime and paint the rack.

After the paint is dry, lay the rack on its front edge and measure and mark shelf placement. Then, stand each shelf on edge within the rack, secure it with a corner clamp and drive nails to fasten it in place. Set the nails and fill the holes.

Make retainers of venetian blind slats nailed to rack sides and shelf bottoms or use ¼-in.-thick lattice.

If possible, snap out the rollers and shafts from their housings. Position the housing on the bottom of the racks so they're within ¼ in. of the edge. Bore a small hole in each end and secure with screws. Snap the rollers and shafts back in and stand the rack upright.

Touch up nail holes with paint and attach the brass pulls. If there is a saddle on the floor below the closet door, remove it so it won't interfere with the rack's mobility.

EACH UNIT is a ¾-in. plywood frame with butt joints. Shelves are ½-in. plywood. Appliance rollers allow unit to move easily and the retainers keep items from falling off pantry shelf. A brass pull lets you pull the unit out of the pantry and return it when you are finished.

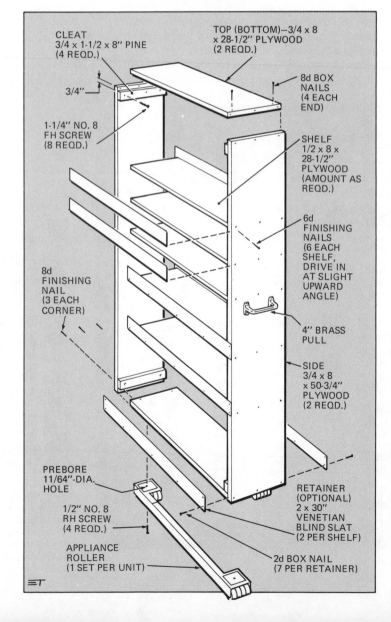

CLEAT
3/4 x 1-1/2 x 8" PINE
(4 REQD.)

3/4"

1-1/4" NO. 8
FH SCREW
(8 REQD.)

8d
FINISHING
NAIL
(3 EACH
CORNER)

PREBORE
11/64"-DIA.
HOLE

1/2" NO. 8
RH SCREW
(4 REQD.)

APPLIANCE
ROLLER
(1 SET PER UNIT)

TOP (BOTTOM)—3/4 x 8
x 28-1/2" PLYWOOD
(2 REQD.)

8d BOX
NAILS
(4 EACH
END)

SHELF
1/2 x 8 x
28-1/2"
PLYWOOD
(AMOUNT AS
REQD.)

6d
FINISHING
NAILS
(6 EACH
SHELF,
DRIVE IN
AT SLIGHT
UPWARD
ANGLE)

4" BRASS
PULL

SIDE
3/4 x 8
x 50-3/4"
PLYWOOD
(2 REQD.)

RETAINER
(OPTIONAL)
2 x 30"
VENETIAN
BLIND SLAT
(2 PER SHELF)

2d BOX NAIL
(7 PER RETAINER)

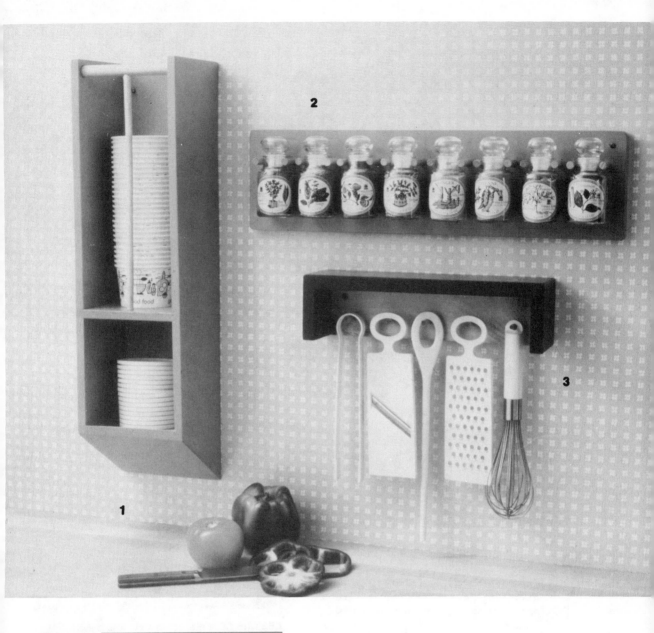

Hang-ups for your kitchen

■ NOWADAYS THE DECORATING preference seems to be to put functional items on a wall—in full view—so they will be handy when needed. The concept works if the items are displayed with a flair that makes them visually pleasing, and these seven projects do just that.

Deli container rack

Lay out and cut all parts as shown in the drawing. Use the miter cut on the bottom of the sides to determine the bevel cut of the front and rear edges of the bottom shelf. Locate the holes for the dowels in the shelf and side pieces and bore them approximately ¼ in. deep. Cut dowels to length and test assemble the rack without glue. When you're satisfied with the fit, disassemble and sand all parts smooth. Using white glue (sparingly) and 1½-in. finishing nails, reassemble the box in this fashion:

● Attach the back to one side (in the rabbet).
● Add the middle and bottom shelves.

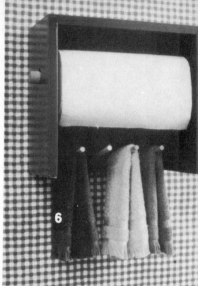

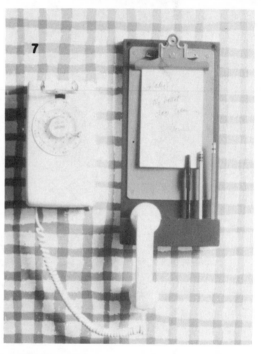

● Insert the longer dowel into the hole bored at the center of the shorter one, then install this T-configuration as a unit into the partial assembly. (Use *glue only* on the dowels.)

● Finally, apply glue where required and fasten the second side.

Using your combination square, check the box for square and set it aside to dry overnight.

Next day, wipe the box with a tack rag, and completely protect the dowels with masking tape. Prime-paint the entire box with a pigmented shellac, or use flat white spray paint as it comes from the can.

Allow the prime coat to dry completely before spraying with the color of your choice.

When the color has dried completely, peel off the masking tape and spray-paint the entire box—dowels and all—with clear varnish.

DESIGNS CONFIRM notion that "less is more." All projects shown are built of ½-in. pine using simple construction throughout.

1 Vertical rack holds a healthy supply of deli containers and lids.

2 Eight spice bottles hang from dowels which are inserted in the pine back.

3 Five-piece kitchen-tool set also hangs from dowels glued into pine backboard.

4 Three-board flowerpot shelf simply rests on window's meeting rail.

5 For safety this knife rack keeps blades close to the wall.

6 This hangup lets you park a large roll of paper towels on a convenient kitchen or bath wall; hand towels are displayed below.

7 Clever clipboard sports a pencil keeper, convenient note pad and a place to park the phone when someone's at the door.

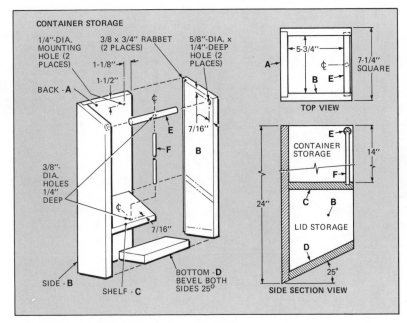

CONTAINER STORAGE

1/4"-DIA. MOUNTING HOLE (2 PLACES)
3/8 x 3/4" RABBET (2 PLACES)
5/8"-DIA. x 1/4"-DEEP HOLE (2 PLACES)
1-1/8"
1-1/2"
BACK - A
E
7/16"
B
3/8"-DIA. HOLES 1/4" DEEP
F
7/16"
SIDE - B
SHELF - C
BOTTOM - D BEVEL BOTH SIDES 25°

A
5-3/4"
7-1/4" SQUARE
B E
TOP VIEW

E
CONTAINER STORAGE
14"
F
24"
C B
LID STORAGE
D
25°
SIDE SECTION VIEW

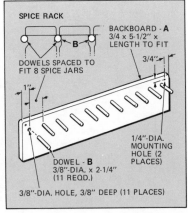

SPICE RACK

BACKBOARD - A 3/4 x 5-1/2" x LENGTH TO FIT
B
DOWELS SPACED TO FIT 8 SPICE JARS
3/4"
1"
1/4"-DIA. MOUNTING HOLE (2 PLACES)
DOWEL - B 3/8"-DIA. x 2-1/4" (11 REQD.)
3/8"-DIA. HOLE, 3/8" DEEP (11 PLACES)

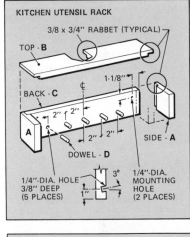

KITCHEN UTENSIL RACK

3/8 x 3/4" RABBET (TYPICAL)
TOP - B
1-1/8"
BACK - C
2" 2"
A
2" 2"
SIDE - A
DOWEL - D
1/4"-DIA. HOLE 3/8" DEEP (5 PLACES)
1"
3°
1/4"-DIA. MOUNTING HOLE (2 PLACES)

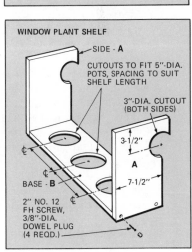

WINDOW PLANT SHELF

SIDE - A
CUTOUTS TO FIT 5"-DIA. POTS, SPACING TO SUIT SHELF LENGTH
3"-DIA. CUTOUT (BOTH SIDES)
3-1/2"
A
BASE - B
7-1/2"
2" NO. 12 FH SCREW, 3/8"-DIA. DOWEL PLUG (4 REQD.)

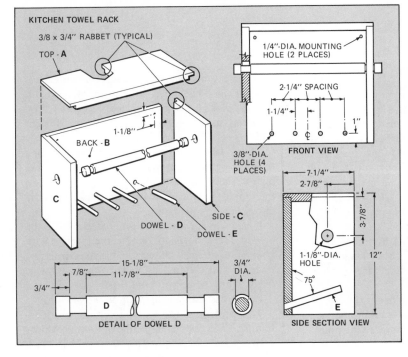

KITCHEN TOWEL RACK

3/8 x 3/4" RABBET (TYPICAL)
TOP - A
1/4"-DIA. MOUNTING HOLE (2 PLACES)
2-1/4" SPACING
1-1/4"
1"
1-1/8"
BACK - B
3/8"-DIA. HOLE (4 PLACES)
FRONT VIEW
C
DOWEL - D
DOWEL - E
SIDE - C
7-1/4"
2-7/8"
3-7/8"
1-1/8"-DIA. HOLE
12"
75°
E
SIDE SECTION VIEW
15-1/8"
7/8"
11-7/8"
3/4"
D
3/4" DIA.
DETAIL OF DOWEL D

MATERIALS LIST—CONTAINER

Key	No.	Size and description (use)
A	1	3/4 × 6½ × 24" (back)
B	2	3/4 × 7¼ × 24" (sides)
C	1	3/4 × 5¾ × 6½" (shelf)
D	1	3/4 × 5¾ × 8" approx., trim to fit (bottom)
E	1	5/8"-dia. × 6¼" (dowel)
F	1	3/8"-dia. × 13⅞" (dowel)
	2	3/16 × 3" toggle bolt

MATERIALS LIST—UTENSIL RACK

Key	No.	Size and description (use)
A	2	3/4 × 3⅛ × 3½" (side)
B	1	3/4 × 3½ × 13½" (top)
C	1	3/4 × 3⅛ × 12¾" (back)
D	1	1/4"-dia. × 1¾" dowel
	2	3/16 × 3" toggle bolts

MATERIALS LIST—SPICE RACK

Key	No.	Size and description (use)
A	1	3/4 × 5½" × length to fit, (back board)
B	11	3/8"-dia. × 2¼" dowel
	2	3/16 × 3" toggle bolt

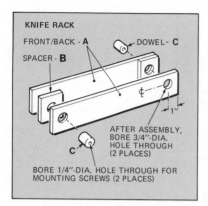

KNIFE RACK

FRONT/BACK - **A**

SPACER - **B**

DOWEL- **C**

¢

1″

AFTER ASSEMBLY,
BORE 3/4″-DIA.
HOLE THROUGH
(2 PLACES)

C

BORE 1/4″-DIA. HOLE THROUGH FOR
MOUNTING SCREWS (2 PLACES)

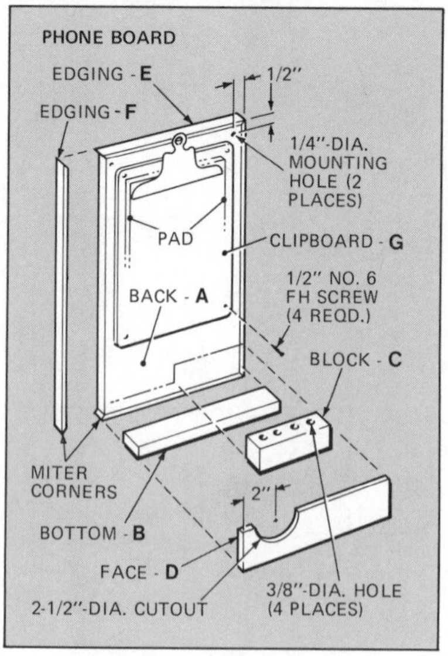

PHONE BOARD

EDGING - **E**

EDGING - **F**

1/2″

1/4″-DIA.
MOUNTING
HOLE (2
PLACES)

PAD

CLIPBOARD - **G**

BACK - **A**

1/2″ NO. 6
FH SCREW
(4 REQD.)

BLOCK - **C**

MITER
CORNERS

BOTTOM - **B**

2″

FACE - **D**

2-1/2″-DIA. CUTOUT

3/8″-DIA. HOLE
(4 PLACES)

MATERIALS LIST—PHONE BOARD

Key	No.	Size and description (use)
A	1	3/4 × 7½ × 15½″ plywood (back)
B	1	3/4 × 1⅛ × 8″ (bottom)
C	1	1⅛ × 1⅛ × 4″ (block)
D	1	1/4 × 1⅞ × 8″ lattice (face)
E	2	1/4 × 3/4 × 8″ lattice (edging, top/bottom)
F	2	1/4 × 3/4 × 16″ lattice (edging, side)
G	1	1/8 × 6½ × 11″ (standard clipboard)
	1	5 × 8″ memo pad
	4	1/2″ No. 6 fh screw
	2	3/16 × 3″ toggle bolt

MATERIALS LIST—TOWEL RACK

Key	No.	Size and description (use)
A	1	3/4 × 7¼ × 13½″ (top)
B	1	3/4 × 11⅝ × 12¾″ (back)
C	2	3/4 × 7¼ × 11⅝″ (side)
D	1	1″-dia. × 15⅛″ dowel
E	4	3/8″-dia. × 6″ dowel

MATERIALS LIST—KNIFE RACK

Key	No.	Size and description (use)
A	2	1/4 × 2¼ × 12″ lattice (front/back)
B	2	1/4 × 2 × 2¼″ lattice (spacer)
C	2	3/4″-dia. × 3/4″ dowel
	2	3/16 × 3″ toggle bolt

MATERIALS LIST—PLANT SHELF

Key	No.	Size and description (use)
A	2	3/4 × 8½ × 12″ (side)
B	1	3/4 × 7½″ × length to suit; see text (shelf)
	4	2″ No. 12 fh screw
	4	3/8″ dowel plug

Spice rack

Start by selecting the type and number of spice bottles that you want to display. Arrange them so you can verify dimensions for the dowel-hole locations. If necessary, adjust the spacing—and length of the board—to suit. At this time, also check dowel length to see if your bottles need more or less dowel.

Bore the dowel holes through. Change bits and bore the pair of holes for hanging. Sand the pieces smooth, dust and tack off.

This piece is easier to finish before assembly. Before spray-painting, insert short lengths of scrap dowel into the holes to protect the surfaces to be glued.

Prime and paint the board. When it's dry, pull out the waste dowels, apply a small amount of glue to dowels (D) and insert them into the holes. Allow to dry overnight. Finish by spraying the entire piece with satin-finish varnish.

Kitchen utensil rack

Cut the four boards to size, as shown in the drawing. Next, set up your saw to cut the 3/8x3/4-in. edge rabbets in the sides and top pieces. Temporarily assemble the pieces and mark where the sidepieces rest on the back (on the inside).

Draw a light pencil line across the front of C (1

in. from the bottom edge) to serve as an aid for locating the dowel holes. To lay out the dowel locations, make a mark at the board's center (L on drawing) and space the dowels 2 in. apart, right and left.

The dowels on the prototype rack were located to suit the equipment to be displayed. To be safe, lay out the actual tools that you plan to hang on the board to check dowel locations. Relocate dowel holes, if necessary.

If you have a steady hand, you can bore the angled blind holes to receive the dowels with your portable drill. Otherwise, tilt your drillpress table 3° and clamp a jig to keep the workpiece from sliding while you bore the row of holes.

Before assembling, sand all pieces smooth.

This project is also easier to paint before assembly. First, test-assemble the box with partially driven nails to make certain you are satisfied with the fit, then disassemble it to apply the finish. Protect all surfaces that will make glue contact by covering them with masking tape.

The dowels can be glued into their holes. Next, board C is wiped with a tack rag and varnished. The board shown received two coats of varnish, with a light sanding between coats.

The sides and top are prime-painted and then sprayed with two coats of a chocolate-brown spray paint.

When the paint is dry, strip off the masking tape and assemble the rack, using white glue (sparingly) and 1½-in. finishing nails. If you assemble in this manner, you will have a mar-free finish: Drive the nails through the back piece into the rabbets in the sides and top. Using wood pads under clamp jaws for protection, clamp the sides into the rabbets at the ends of the top piece.

Window plant shelf

Start by checking the window size where you plan to use this shelf. As can be seen in the photograph, the unit hangs from the "¾-moon" cutouts which simply rest on a double-hung window's meeting rail. The vertical sides bear against the window stiles beneath the meeting rail. So measure from center to center of the stiles of your window, and use this dimension for the *outside* (overall length) dimension of your shelf.

Cut all three parts to size. Then, using nails in the waste area, tack both sides together. Cut both sides to shape at one time, using either band or sabre saw.

Refer to the actual pots to be displayed to lay out the holes in the shelf. Use a compass to scribe the circle diameters and cut the holes out using a sabre saw. Check all holes for fit with the pots before proceeding.

Assemble the shelf, using 8d (2½-in.) finishing nails and white glue.

When it's dry, mask the shelf (B), using tape and newspapers. Prime and paint the sides with the color of your choice (a burnt orange was used on the prototype). When the paint is dry, remove masking materials and apply two coats of varnish to all surfaces.

Knife rack

Before cutting out the four wood pieces, lay out the collection of knives that you intend to display. Adjust rack length if necessary.

Assemble the pieces using glue, and clamp the pieces overnight. Next day, when glue is dry, remove the clamps and secure the joints by driving several ⅝-in. brads through the back and spacer into the front. Do this at both ends. Make certain brads aren't driven where the dowel holes must be bored.

The walnut dowels are actually just for looks. Locate them and bore neat, round holes. Using glue sparingly, install the dowels.

Sand all exposed surfaces smooth, dust and wipe with a tack cloth. Finish with two or three coats of spray varnish.

Kitchen towel rack

This case is assembled by using the same construction as for other hanging cases.

First, cut the parts to size. Next, to bore the towel bar holes, clamp the sides together and bore both at one time. Lay out and bore the holes for the dowels and assemble the box.

Insert scrap pieces of dowel into the dowel holes to protect gluing surfaces from the paint. Sand the box smooth, prime and paint with the color of your choice. We used blue spray paint on the case shown.

Cut the towel bar to length and mark for the grooves upon which the bar rides the sides. To cut the grooves, use your miter gauge and table saw.

Raise the saw blade to cut to a depth of ⅛ in. and, slowly and carefully, rotate the dowel to make the cuts.

You can use a conventional blade and make a series of overlapping cuts. Or you can install the dado head, set up to cut a ⅞-in.-wide groove. The first method takes longer, but you might feel more comfortable doing it.

Test the bar for fit; when you're satisfied, apply two coats of varnish to it.

Glue the ⅜-in. dowels in place and set the unit aside to dry overnight. Next day, apply one or two coats of varnish. Sand the first coat lightly when dry, then dust with a tack cloth before applying the second.

Phone board

For this project, start by buying the clipboard and memo pad because the backup board (A) is sized to suit the clipboard.

Cut the three parts that make up the tray at bottom, and drill all the pencil holes in C. Sand these parts before fastening them to the backup board.

Miter-cut the edging and fasten it to the plywood board, using white glue (sparingly) and brads.

Locate the clipboard on A and bore pilot holes through for the screws. Countersink the holes in the clipboard and remove it from the phone board.

Dust all pieces and wipe with a tack cloth. Apply prime paint to all surfaces. (*Note:* If you use spray paint, plug the pencil holes first.) Paint the phone and clipboards in the colors of your choice. When the paint is dry, mount the clipboard, using flathead brass screws, or apply dabs of paint to the screwheads.

Easy projects add spice to your kitchen

OLD-TIME GROCERY-BIN CANISTER

SILVERWARE-AND-NAPKIN CADDY

■ YOU'LL FIND lots of use for this silverware and napkin caddy—it's extra-handy when serving a buffet meal. Except for the turned handle, the caddy is made of ½-in. walnut throughout. Both ends are identical and cut out at one time, the holes bored for the handle and the edges rounded. With the turned handle in place, the ends are fastened squarely to the center member with small screws in counterbored holes, later filled. Then the bottom is added.

The two dividers are made to fit the round edge of the center piece by forming a ¼-in.-radius lip at the top with a round file. They're screwed in place from the back. The two slanting sides are added last. The caddy is finished with Danish-walnut stain, followed by two coats of clear satin polyurethane.

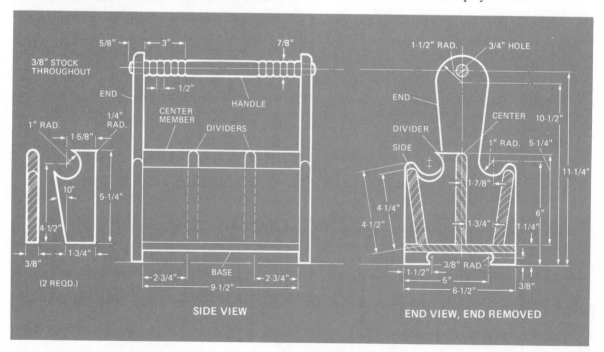

SIDE VIEW

END VIEW, END REMOVED

Grocery-bin canister

This miniature version of an oldtime grocery-store bin will add a charming accent to your kitchen in the form of a five-in-one canister. It's made to hold half-gallon plastic food containers you can buy in housewares departments. You have the option of making five separate lids or a one-piecer that looks like five. The window openings are made in one strip.

Windows are cut out by drilling ⅜-in. holes at corners of the openings, then jigsawing from hole to hole. Rabbets for 1/10-in. Plexiglas are formed with ⅛-in. thick strips. Use dabs of quick-setting epoxy to hold the plastic in place.

OLD TIME GROCERY-BIN CANISTER

BUTT-JOIN, glue and nail ¼-in. bottom to the six compartment dividers.

DOUBLE-UP top's thickness with second ¼-in. layer beveled at the front.

USE homemade sander in jigsaw to smooth the window openings' edges.

FORM rabbets for window panes by adding ⅛-in. strips around openings.

HALF-GALLON plastic food containers are placed in the compartments.

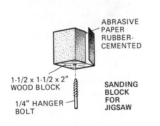

HANGER bolt in abrasive-covered block is chucked in jigsaw for sanding.

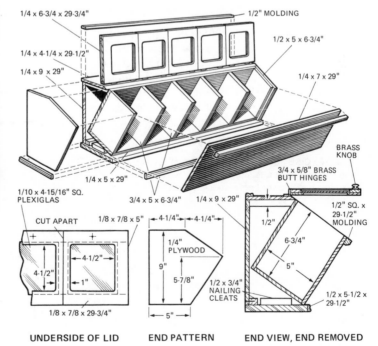

UNDERSIDE OF LID   END PATTERN   END VIEW, END REMOVED

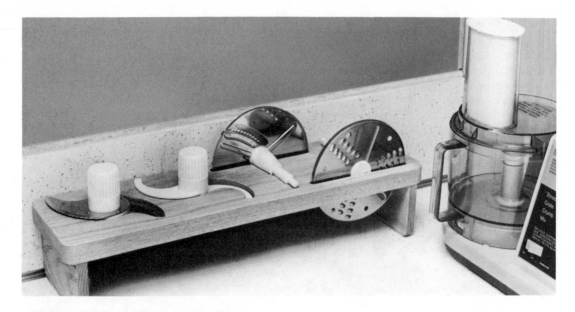

Rack for food-processor parts

■ STORE FOOD-PROCESSOR parts neatly and conveniently on hand in this accessory rack. Since the rack shelf consists of two pieces glued together, you can make the odd-shaped cutouts with a saw rather than carving or routing them. Make sure you select perfectly flat wood to facilitate joining.

Cut the four pieces needed. Use your processor parts as guides to outline the cutouts. Then bore entry holes for the saw blade in the cutouts: six in the top piece and four in the bottom one. Position holes for the long slots at the cutout ends.

Use a jigsaw or coping saw, making the cutouts slightly larger than the accessories to assure an easy fit. Use half-round and flat wood files, then sand smooth.

Glue shelf sections together and secure parts with finishing nails from below. When the glue has dried, cut the shelf corners round, break the edges with a plane and sand smooth.

Attach the legs with glue and finishing nails. Set the heads below the surface and use plastic wood filler. Apply polyurethane varnish.

FOR PRECISE cutouts (right, top photo), use set-tooth blade. For parts fit, remove line when cutting. Use two nails (lower photo) to align parts. Apply glue sparingly, and then nail.

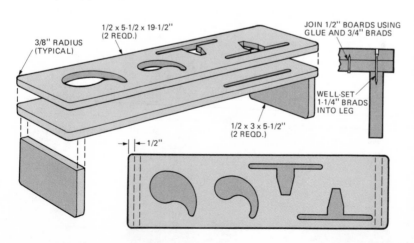

3/8" RADIUS (TYPICAL)

1/2 x 5-1/2 x 19-1/2" (2 REQD.)

JOIN 1/2" BOARDS USING GLUE AND 3/4" BRADS

WELL-SET 1-1/4" BRADS INTO LEG

1/2 x 3 x 5-1/2" (2 REQD.)

1/2"

Tray for your best silver

■ THE HANDSOME TRAY pictured here looks complicated to make, but it's actually very easy. Constructed of ⅜-in. poplar, this attractive silverware holder is basically simple in design and construction. Though assembly ordinarily would be difficult (because of the tray's angular sides), it's a snap here because of a simple gluing jig that eliminates otherwise difficult clamping.

Start by laying out the patterns on a sheet of heavy paper, then cut them out with scissors or a razor blade. Using the templates as a blade-setting guide, set the table-saw blade to coincide with the angle of the patterns and rip one edge of lumber at this angle. Cut enough to make up the two sides and two end panels. After the bevel has been cut, return the blade to the 0° setting.

Align the bottom edge of the pattern with the beveled edge of the wood and trace the outline. Do this for ends and sides. The divider is traced onto a square piece of wood. All parts are cut on the jigsaw. The gluing jig, with its beveled cutout, simply slips over the assembled tray and holds the parts together until dry. After the glue has set, remove the piece from the jig and glue on the bottom. Finish the tray with stain and two coats of shellac.

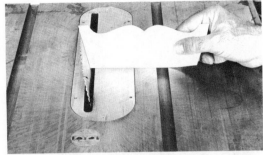

MAKE THE templates and set the blade to the right angle for ripping the edges of the sides and ends.

THE SCROLLS are cut on a jigsaw. For a smooth cut use a very fine blade, high speed and a slow feed.

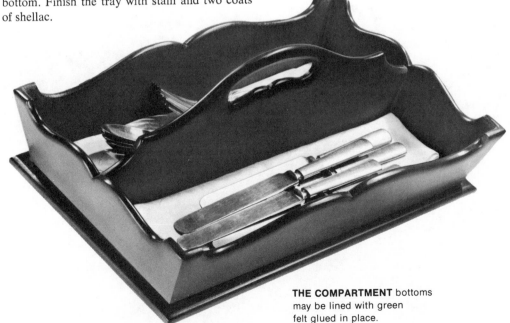

THE COMPARTMENT bottoms may be lined with green felt glued in place.

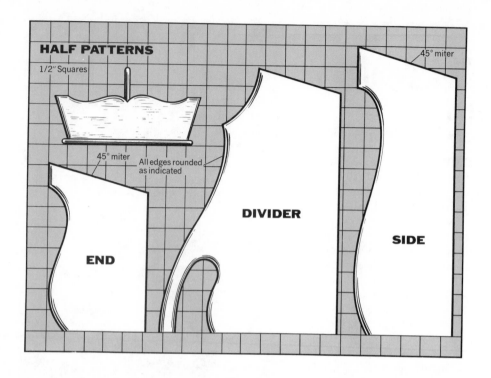

HALF PATTERNS

1/2" Squares

45° miter

END

45° miter

All edges rounded
as indicated

DIVIDER

45° miter

SIDE

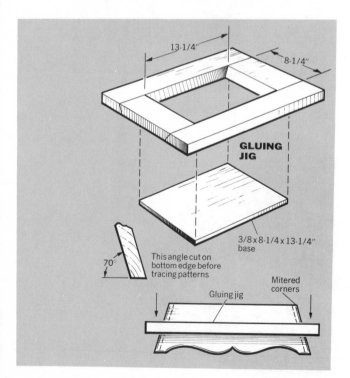

13-1/4"

8-1/4"

GLUING JIG

3/8 x 8-1/4 x 13-1/4"
base

70°

This angle cut on
bottom edge before
tracing patterns

Gluing jig

Mitered
corners

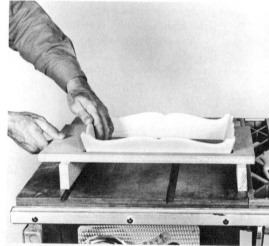

THE GLUING jig consists of a piece of plywood with a
beveled cutout. No nails are used in the assembly.

Turned-handle cutting board

■ HERE'S A PROJECT you can turn out in a few hours—though it will last a lifetime. Start by preparing a 1½-in.-thick piece of cherry, rock maple or walnut and a full-sized cardboard template. Center the template accurately on the hardwood slab and mark the outline. Drill 1-in. holes at the base of the handle, then cut the blank to shape with a sabre saw or a bandsaw.

Find the precise center of the blank and mount it in the lathe, being sure both centers are set deeply into the end grain of the wood. Keep the lathe speed slow—about 900 rpm. Start cutting with a gouge at midpoint, working away from the board toward the handle end. Make successive cuts in this direction, starting each bite closer to the base of the handle.

To blend the handle with the flat blank, hold the gouge on its side with its handle nearly parallel with the sloped slides. As you slice in, roll the gouge flat and toward the handle end. Finish turning the handle with gouge and skew, then sand it smooth with strips of 120-grit paper.

Now remove the work from the lathe and sand the rough-sawn edges on a disc sander. Drill and countersink the hole for the leather loop and give the flat surfaces a thorough sanding with 100 and 120-grit paper. Finish with two or three coats of linseed oil and a coat of paraffin dissolved in mineral spirits. Thread a 24-in. length of rawhide boot lace through the handle and knot it.

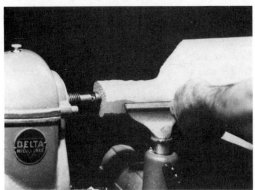

USE A ¾-in. gouge to begin turning handle section round. Keep hands clear of whirring blank.

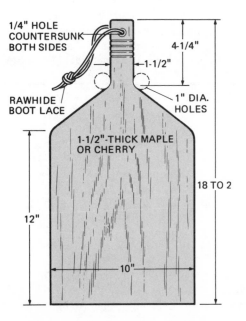

1/4" HOLE COUNTERSUNK BOTH SIDES

4-1/4"

1-1/2"

RAWHIDE BOOT LACE

1" DIA. HOLES

1-1/2"-THICK MAPLE OR CHERRY

18 TO 2

12"

10"

Telephone organizer

■ THIS HANDSOME MAHOGANY cabinet is a smart way to store phone equipment in your kitchen or home office, library or den while providing valuable storage space. The dimensions can be altered easily to conform to your specific equipment.

Make the cabinet from mahogany hardwood; use ¼-in. lauan mahogany plywood for the cabinet back and drawer bottom. Start by cutting the cabinet sides to the dimensions given. Mahogany is commonly available in 16-in.-wide boards, but you can edge-glue two boards together to form each side.

Rout stopped dadoes into the sides using a router and a straight bit to accept the horizontal cross members. Then chisel the rounded ends of the dadoes square. Cut the top shelf and cabinet bottom to size and rabbet the back edges of both to accept the cabinet back. Note that the front corners of the shelf are notched to extend past dadoes. Rout decorative profile in the front edge of the top shelf using a ¼-in.-rad. cove bit.

Make the frame to support the pullout tray. Assemble frame with half-lap joints and then slot the four inside corners as shown for the tray-stop screws. Dry-assemble the cabinet with clamps so you can fit the doors properly.

The doors operate on invisible barrel or cylinder hinges inserted into 14-mm-dia. holes bored into the door edge and cabinet side. The 14-mm-dia. drill bit is available from the hinge supplier. First, bore hinge holes into the doors, then insert ½-in.-dia. dowel centers (wrap the dowel centers with masking tape so they fit snugly into the holes). Next, press each door against the cabinet side so the dowel center points transfer the hinge hole centers to the cabinet sides. Disassemble the cabinet and bore the hinge holes. Then use the ¼-in.-rad. cove bit to rout the edges of the sides and doors as shown. Reassemble and clamp the cabinet using glue only.

Assemble and install the drawer. Before nailing the cabinet back, mark rear slot locations against the underside of the pullout tray. Bore pilot holes at these two marks for the tray-stop screws. Apply three coats of polyurethane varnish to all parts. Then nail on the back and install the pullout tray. Use an offset screwdriver to turn in the tray-stop screws.

THIS MAHOGANY home office organizer holds an office-model phone and answering machine; has storage drawer, cabinet, and pullout writing surface. It provides a lot of storage—all in only 1½ sq. ft. of floor space.

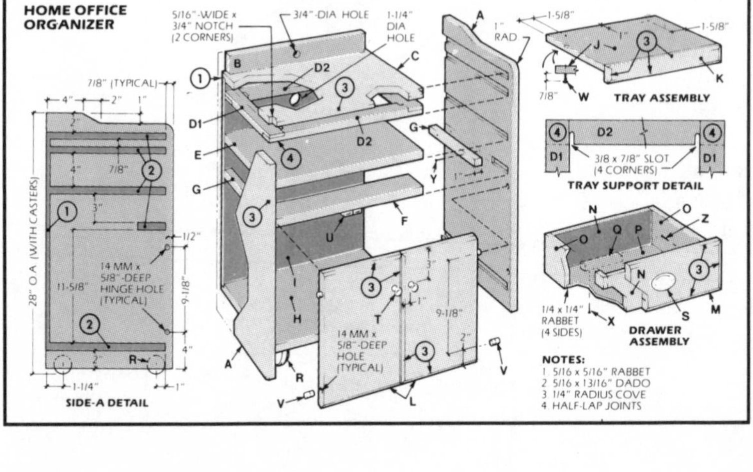
HOME OFFICE ORGANIZER
SIDE-A DETAIL
TRAY ASSEMBLY
TRAY SUPPORT DETAIL
3/8 x 7/8" SLOT (4 CORNERS)
DRAWER ASSEMBLY
1/4 x 1/4" RABBET (4 SIDES)
14 MM x 5/8"-DEEP HINGE HOLE (TYPICAL)
28" O.A. (WITH CASTERS)
NOTES:
1 5/16 x 5/16" RABBET
2 5/16 x 13/16" DADO
3 1/4" RADIUS COVE
4 HALF-LAP JOINTS

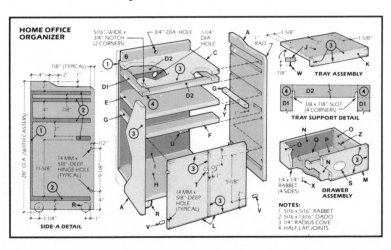

MATERIALS LIST

HOME OFFICE TELEPHONE ORGANIZER

Key	No.	Size and description (use)
A	2	13/16 x 14 x 27½" mahogany (side)
B	1	13/16 x 2 x 14½" mahogany (upper back)
C	1	13/16 x 13⅞ x 15" mahogany (top)
D1	2	13/16 x 1¾ x 12¾" mahogany (side rail)
D2	2	13/16 x 1¾ x 15" mahogany (front and rear rail)
E	1	13/16 x 12¾ x 15" mahogany (shelf)
F	1	13/16 x 3 x 15" mahogany (cabinet rail)
G	2	¾ x 1 x 9¾" mahogany (drawer guide)
H	2	13/16 x 13⅞ x 15" mahogany (bottom)
I	1	¼ x 15 x 22¾" lauan plywood (back)
J	1	13/16 x 12 11/16 x 14 5/16" mahogany (pullout tray)
K	1	13/16 x 1¾ x 14⅜" mahogany (tray front)
L	2	13/16 x 7⅛ x 13¼" mahogany (door)
M	1	13/16 x 3 13/16 x 14 5/16" mahogany (drawer face)
N	2	½ x 2⅞ x 13 5/16" mahogany (drawer front and back)
O	2	½ x 2⅞ x 12⅝" mahogany (drawer side)
P	1	¼ x 12⅛ x 13 13/16" lauan plywood (drawer bottom)
Q	1	¾ x ¾ x 5" mahogany (drawer stop)
R	4	2" plate-type casters
S	1	2" brass pull
T	2	1"-dia. brass knob
U	2	Magnetic catch
V	4	Invisible barrel hinge
W	2	1½" No. 14 roundhead screw (tray stop)
X	2	1½" No. 6 flathead screw (drawer stop)
Y		1½" finishing nails
Z		1" brads